EMBODY PRESENCE

The New

FEMININE
EVOLUTIONARY

FLOWER OF LIFE PRESS.
Voices of Transformation

Cover Artwork by Shiloh Sophia
Book design by Jane Ashley

To contact the publisher, visit
FLOWEROFLIFEPRESS.COM

Library of Congress Control Number: 2017912959
Flower of Life Press, Lyme, CT.

ISBN-13: 978-0-9863539-2-5

Printed in the United States of America

CANTOS OF RECLAMATION

Red, gold, orange, crimson, umber—forging an environment of sacred fire and chaos. Next is the mapping out sacred geometry on a piece of wood I have had for more than nine years. Marking out Fibonaci spirals, Vesica piscis, and seeds of life blooming. I draw them by hand so the organic nature of creation is held here, even though I know it will disappear in the layers. It will always be there. Underneath what we see, there is another world. The journey begins with a prayer. Weaving together the energies and stories of twenty-two women speaking.

This act of Intentional Creativity is sparked by inquiry of the heart and the blessing of the wood. How do I create an image of the feminine that is both ancient and of the future? How do I include dark and light, and yet not be dualistic and obvious? How do I include the energy of the Priestess who may serve the old ways and the new ways and weave them together? Could I include many nationalities somehow? How do I tell my own story in the painting, while telling the story of all of us? How do we transcend duality and move into unity, but not be as if it's all good all the time? Could I have a bit of "Mona Lisa" in the image, where we wonder what she's thinking? Can we be catalyzed while we look at it?

I painted many days with tea and late night by candlelight with kitties and red wine and music, my lover reading me poetry when I was tired. I finished the painting during the eclipse. The blooming of her consciousness with wings on her head. The top is the constellation of the future, the bottom has water at the base with a root system: heaven and earth. All the elements are present. The pomegranate is the collective heart and, if you look closely, an ancient Blessed Mother is in the center and there is a small flame at the top, hope for humanity. A dark and light side of her face and the mystical roses for integration. The glowing red mantle for the Priestess going about her sacred work. The eclipse and many moons in which she is the center, forming a new archetype for evolution. Her earrings, one with sacred geometry of the feminine/earth and a Celtic Cross/medicine wheel on the other side. Honeycomb code on one side with bees, and on the other side binary code to represent our relationship with technology as sacred.

This is her, yet it is a collective feminine in the midst singing her Cantos for Reclamation. She sings for herself, while she sings for all of us.

Acrylic on Wood
Shiloh Sophia,
August 21, 2017

Cantos of Reclamation

She is the quickening
Standing at the threshold of now

She doesn't perform alchemy
She is the embodied alchemical process

She doesn't need to create legacy by design
She IS the legacy, as it reveals itself

She certainly isn't waiting to be discovered
The Lady has already discovered herself!

She is not persuaded by readings of the almost future
That hold prophecies of prescribed delivery or doom

She carries the codes of the tree of life in her blood
She prays to be ready to receive the fullness of the teachings

She need not constantly seek to heal what is wounded
She carries holy wholeness in her unbroken soul

With supple shimmer, she slips out of stories worn old
Gliding from hidden worlds into the joy of pure presence

She is woven of the 'matter' of mysterious darkness
A daughter of Wisdom, whose radiance never ceases

She is at the intersection where light enters the prism
Surrendering unnecessary struggle, heralding an age of beauty

Her true lover is not her opposite, nor her reflection,
What they are, who they are, is still being in-formed

She is one of the many messengers of the ancient future
First re-membering, and then creating with intention

She is a shelter for the sacred, a call to action for the lost
The revealing of an archetype from the celestial eclipse

Her creativity, marks out the atlas of possibility
Dissolving duality, tending to reclamation and refuge

Where paths meet she takes her stand, a vesica piscis view
weaving technology and biology as stardust methodology

She knows from whence the gifts come, from the Creator,
She chooses the narrow path of the one called The Way

The lineage she carries is carried by all people
Yet often lays hidden under suppression of consciousness

She calls a council to gather, Mystics, Poets, Painters,
Cantors, Scientists, Dancers, Wisdom Keepers and Christos Seekers

As an initiation they reclaim language, image, code, seed and sound
A new mythos is revealed, already carried in the codex of the soul

Together they explore the intersections that have divided us
Offering up a view of generosity, prosperity and justice

She shrugs off continual apology for self and projections from others
With acceptance and forgiveness for self and others, she emerges

She steps out of systems of any kind that do not support life
Simultaneously stepping into structures of divine design

She is the scribe and curator of her own becoming
Guided by her call to the ministry of refuge and reclamation

She accepts with gravity, her responsibility to the great unfolding
Nurturing herself, she discovers the nurturing for those she serves

Her unreasonable prayer is a song for the wellness of all
An offering of love, comfort and an invitation to the quickening

She hopes that this reading may be a Blessing for you,
as it has been for Her, in the writing and the revelation.

The writing of one's own Cantos of Reclamation
can be a ritual towards the awakening.

~Shiloh Sophia

CONTENTS

DEDICATION

I dedicate this book to my daughters, Ruby, Penelope, Annabella, and Sadie ... may you always find the light in the darkness and remember that you are love and loved—in All Ways and Always.

ACKNOWLEDGMENTS

My heart is full of gratitude—thank you to all of the authors in this book for bringing forth your truest essence, courage, and willingness to be of service and create positive change in our world. I honor and love you, sisters of my heart.

Thank you to our cover artist and author Shiloh Sophia for your compassion and support in providing such a magnificent representation of the New Feminine Evolutionary for our cover. She takes my breath away.

Thank you to Amy Paradysz for your wonderful copy editing. Amy, you are a vital part of this team and we are grateful for your keen eye and diligent support.

Thank you to my husband Scott Watrous, Chief Strategist of Flower of Life Press, for your unending love and willingness to hold me to the fire as we brought this project through and to fruition. Thank you for bringing this book to her highest vibration so that she resonates in truth and authenticity.

And, finally, I am in deep gratitude to Mother Earth and this precious life that we share—to the Divine Mother in each of us who carries humanity forward as we create a legacy of grace, abundance, and limitless love.

~Jane Ashley

Introduction

BY JANE ASHLEY, *PUBLISHER*

Something had been pulling at me and I couldn't quite put my finger on it. It seemed that since Trump took office, so much fear was in the air and there was a ton of static in our collective energy. Clients, colleagues and sisters were reflecting back a new sense of urgency and desire for action. *What can we do? How can we change so that humanity can move forward rather than backwards? How can we turn towards love, stay in our sovereignty and make a difference? How can we be inclusive of All of Life and heal the wounds both personally and collectively?*

I'd asked these questions before … we all have, right? Something felt different, though. The old ways weren't working anymore—not in our relationships, not in our ways of communicating, not in our soul-based businesses. The heat was turning up—fast. Everything was shifting so quickly, faster than I could keep up with most days, and I'd been feeling so pushed and ungrounded due to my crazy schedule and harried life.

I was circling around the knowing that something new was on the horizon, a vibration that tugged at me like some primordial urge forward, up, out of the ooze of my own story towards … a new me.

Evolution takes time.

The night the idea for this book came through, I was in a state of opening to receive guidance from Source about our next collaborative book project for Flower of Life Press. My usual way of receiving "the big idea" was to engage in inquiry with my husband Scott about what was up in the field, and then go into silence to open up in surrender and receive guidance from Source.

We focused our talk on the craziness all around us—and the challenges we face as divine expressions of the feminine/masculine energies. *How can we adapt and thrive in the midst of chaos? What is our path?*

TWO DAYS LATER

I hopped in my car and took off to teach a class not far from my home. Before I knew it,

CRASH!

I had driven myself right into a tree, two hundred yards from my driveway. The tree was rotten, and the impact caused it to crack in half and land on the windshield. All I remember is feeling the impact, crashing glass all around, the smell of smoke from the airbags, and the sound of the blaring horn.

Adrenaline was rushing as I pushed open the crumpled car door and stepped out wide-eyed and stunned. The car was totaled. I couldn't believe that I had walked right out of there, unscathed other than a little bruising and lots of shock.

I looked at that broken tree and fell to my knees in gratitude. *Thank you, thank you, thank you.*

Gratitude turned instantly into judgment: I was so angry at myself and fell into instant shame.

Now we need a new car, which is a huge expense ... I can't teach my class and I have twenty people waiting for me! The monkey mind took over. My sixteen-year-old daughter had just gotten her license the day before. *What will my family think? Will they judge me? What is WRONG with me?!*

I heard the sirens coming to the scene from the firehouse just up the road. The neighbors had gathered, brought water and were doing their best to comfort me. Shaking, I called my husband.

As I looked at the cacophony around me, I saw a dead bird lying in the middle of the road. It was a mama Flicker bird who'd obviously been living in the tree that I just hit—and her eggs lay shattered around her broken body. I felt a wave of tears let loose. *How could I have killed that poor bird and her babies? And I ruined that beautiful tree!* My heart was broken.

I knew there was medicine here for me. Later, when I looked up the spiritual meaning of the Flicker bird, I found that she represents a new rhythm and cycle of growth; she activates our intuition and changes our perceptions. She shows the importance of healing love and the power of forgiveness, and emphasizes tenacity, patience, and action. She teaches us how to connect with the earth and how to ground ourselves in nature. Flicker helps us find deeper meanings and hidden qualities of patterns and coincidences. She teaches balance and harmony in the spiritual and mental realms.

Umm … yeah! An awareness spread through me—I had found my way back into old masculine patterns of going, going, going until I was completely burned out and not present in my life. So much so that a tree and a Flicker bird needed to show how me to *STOP. Get Grounded. Stop running. Be Here Now.*

And then, the idea came crashing in, just like the car had hit the tree. This book needs to share how we must BECOME THE CHANGE before we "crash and total" our nervous systems, not to mention all of humanity and the earth—from utter lack of presence and embodiment.

We must evolve—women and men, sovereign beings connected to each other and our sacred Gaia. We must embody evolution—or we will perish in our own fire.

······⌾⫯⌾······

In my experience, writing is a transformative journey and, upon saying YES to the opportunity, will likely bring forward some deep initiations for the writer. Fierce initiations into a deeper heart space of self-love, worthiness, visibility, ability to receive, and so many more. That's the whole point of evolution, right? To be able to release our old patterns and stories and write new ones that resonate in truth. To raise our vibration and be present in each moment.

For the past few years, a common meme has been shared via social media that is believed to be the words of Gandhi: "Be the change you wish to see in the world." But as Joseph Ranseth (josephranseth.com) shares, that's not exactly how Gandhi phrased it—even though the meaning is there. Here's the actual quote from Mahatma Gandhi:

> "We but mirror the world. All the tendencies present in the outer world are to be found in the world of our body. If we could change ourselves, the tendencies in the world would also change. As a man changes his own nature, so does the attitude of the world change towards him. This is the divine mystery supreme. A wonderful thing it is and the source of our happiness. We need not wait to see what others do."

Ranseth points out that the idea of "Be the change you wish to see in the world" does three powerful things when we adopt it:

1. It stops us from judging others;
2. It replaces complaining about others with reflection on self;
3. It stirs us into taking action within the only thing in the world over which we have any control: ourselves.

These three statements are the purpose and mission of this book, and the reason for the tagline *Embody Presence—Become the Change.* The twenty-two radical feminine evolutionary writers who joined me on this journey dared to be vulnerable. They share their voices as a mirror for you, dear reader. The courageous act of writing with transparency and a willingness to step out and be seen in our sovereignty is what is required of all of us … NOW. These fractious times require it.

All it takes is one pin prick of light to change the trajectory of a person's life. My wish is that the words in this book will create that opening for you so that the vibration of love will permeate you and ripple out to your families, communities, and beyond.

On this journey, you too, will Become the Change, and dance with the Divine Feminine as she shows up in your life.

The Realization That Changes Everything

BY ALIA

There is a common experience we go through as human beings: We experience multiple life initiations and moments of hitting bottom that have the potential to open us to healing and transcendence if we let them.

Then there is a point we can reach when it has gone far enough. When all the days that have passed feeling disconnected from ourselves becomes too much to bear. When the gnawing on our insides at how much things are out of alignment becomes too loud to ignore. When all the symptoms—the pain in our body, the depression, the gripping sadness, the vast emptiness—are undeniable.

The suffering can be immense and can take some of the strongest warriors down.

Sometimes, though, these initiations can open us to some of the most significant insights necessary to help us alchemize our pain and discover how to thrive on our life journey.

What often follows is that moment when everything comes to a head, when we hear the soft whispers of our inner knowing and we decide, "I have to change this."

I have found my way through many initiatory moments. I have worked through multiple rapes and sexual abuse, the fallout from an angry narcissistic father, intense financial stress, an eating disorder, big healing crises, a divorce, and my brother's death, to name a few.

Every one of these passages required immense strength. I've discovered that, if we are paying attention, we can find the signs that we are being held through even the greatest suffering.

I recognized this for the first time about thirteen years ago when I sat on a mountain alone on a traditional Native American vision quest with no food and water for four days.

I had hiked up a steep mountain with my guide to be left alone at my spot in an isolated clearing, barely able to make it up because I had mysteriously lost full use of one leg a few months earlier.

For months leading up to the quest, I had been in great pain and quite scared that it was going to stay that way because none of the experts seemed to know what was wrong. This was impacting everything in my life from my marriage to my career, and the fear was getting to me. I was facing the possibility of losing my mobility, something of great value to me, and it shook me to the core.

On my vision quest everything that was painful in my body became inflamed to the point that I couldn't sleep. I was so stripped down after days of this (combined with no water and food which, frankly, was the best part of the whole experience) that I finally gave in and screamed in agony, "Please help me!"

I didn't know if anything or anyone was even hearing me. For most of my young adult life I had been disillusioned by the teachings I heard at church and for years I'd felt disconnected from God. I carried the belief that I alone had to shoulder everything that happened to me, which often left me feeling overwhelmed by my challenges.

Despite my lack of belief, I kept sobbing and repeating, "Please help me" over and over like a mantra. After hours of this with no relief, I started to think it was futile.

Then I received a sign—a hummingbird zoomed over my shoulder right by my ear, flipped around, and hovered in front of my face. That ten seconds or so it was in front of me slowed into eternity and I filled with the recognition that I had been heard. Something softened in me. I knew perhaps for the first time in my life that I *wasn't* alone.

After the vision quest, my physical strength returned and my inner strength grew. I became a spiritual seeker searching for the consistent connection to what I had experienced. This led me first to deepen in Native

American traditions. Not surprisingly, my elder George, who I found many years after my quest, teaches that the best simple prayer to Creator is, "Please help me!"—the prayer I had cried out on the mountain.

At the same time, I began reawakening my connection to my feminine, which inspired me to want to understand my spiritual path as a woman, specifically. I recognized that it felt more true to me to name that connection I felt years prior "Goddess." I became initiated as a priestess with a mystery school and it became obvious that I am here to be an Ambassador for Her, the Grand SHE.

For a long time, I related to Her as something outside of me. What I didn't realize yet, that I came to understand more recently, is that I AM HER.

At the time of this writing, the collective has been going through a hit-bottom moment since the 2017 U.S. election. Many of us felt shock and despair when Donald Trump was made President. He ushered in an era marked by repression, lies, misogyny, and narcissism.

We are seeing the emergence of a violent extreme right faction emboldened by Trump's election. We are seeing attempts to roll back environmental protections and progressive laws we had taken for granted would be held sacred in a democratic country. We are seeing how fast the tide can turn and how quickly our freedoms can be stripped away. We have become present to the fragile, tenuous state of affairs. It has ushered in a deepening commitment to make our voices heard.

Just after the election, I felt a hopelessness and fear come over me that I hadn't felt in a long time.

Then I found myself becoming ever more committed to creating change. Like so many, I began asking, "What can I do?"

We know that for thousands of years women have lived through the age of patriarchy that has systematically subjugated us. But, more recently, we have also been seeing a feminine movement sweeping the planet. In women's empowerment circles we have been reclaiming the Divine Feminine within us. We speak of the return of feminine leadership and of the new feminine evolutionary that is being awoken from her slumber. We are coming together to remember the truth of who we are.

For over a decade I have been helping to empower women through my projects Femvolution™ and Feminine Medicine™. This year, however, something was calling me to go even deeper. I felt there was a missing link

I wanted to speak to, and I began to receive a new body of work that I have been offering women who I mentor in my community Creatrix Collective™. I want to share a piece of what I have discovered here with you.

The Dalai Lama declared, "The world will be saved by the Western woman," likely because Western women have comparatively more opportunities, education, and resources, so therefore a greater chance of creating change. Despite better odds, though, Western women are still suffering. Many of us have been caught in the spell cast by society that makes us believe that we are powerless to create change. This is even true for some of us who have had a privileged life and an abundance of financial resources.

We struggle with low confidence and self-esteem and don't believe in ourselves and our ideas. We hate our bodies. We doubt ourselves. We allow ourselves to be taken advantage of. We get taken out by negative thoughts or self-sabotaging behaviors that keep us from moving forward.

Many of us have trouble seeing ourselves as worthy of love, of money, or even of happiness. We often don't see a pathway to be fully self-expressed and free. We don't know how to change our circumstances, and we can't see a way to live our creative purpose or a life that fulfills us.

We experience a deep soul-level pain that manifests as despair, depression, self-criticism, and self-betrayal that convinces us that we aren't good enough or that we don't have it in us to manifest the ideas and visions that live inside of us. We have forgotten who we are and what we are truly capable of.

In some parts of the world today, women are still not allowed to speak, work, drive, vote, or show their faces. Women and girls are traded and sold into slavery or have their sexual organs mutilated to prevent them from experiencing pleasure. Even in our country, women are still not paid equally.

No wonder so many of us struggle! Most of us were not given the blueprint for how to create in a world that is not supportive of our self-expression and that has been censoring women for centuries.

One of the most heartbreaking symptoms of this is our fear of sharing our voices. This shows up in our relationships and family dynamics, and it has perhaps the greatest impact in our careers. For some women, the fear is so gripping that the fullest possible expression of our life-changing work is never shared. For years I struggled with the fear of speaking in front of others and especially with putting my voice to my songs. Today I lead large groups and sing on major stages, but it was a battle, and the victory was hard won.

Sister, do you see yourself in any of this?

If so, you are in good company. I have worked with hundreds of women, and I can tell you that most of us struggle with some of these things every day.

We are fighting our way through. Some of us can spend decades doing clearing work and still sense that there is a way that we are not quite as expressed as we know we could be. Some of the most visible female leaders I know still struggle with a lot of what I have described here too.

It is difficult to create big shifts at a collective level when sometimes it feels like we are still fighting ourselves!

So how can we move through this?

Take this in.

I meditated on this for a long time asking to be shown the missing link. This is what my higher consciousness said:

You are the Creatrix and you have the power to create your reality.

Creatrix is the feminine form of Creator and another name for the feminine face of God, the Goddess, Source, the Universe, or whatever word resonates for you. The Creatrix is the generative Source of all creation and lies within you and all beings. She is the feminine impulse that gave everything form and life.

When you come to the realization that you ARE the Creatrix, it is the realization that changes everything!

Why?

This happens when we wake up to the Creatrix within:

We see ourselves as a divine being.
We take total responsibility for our sovereignty.
We recognize our power.
We see that we can choose.
We decide how it's going to be.
The truth is what we say it is.
The limiting thoughts and ideas fall away.
We come to a place of trust.
We see our magnificence.
Life becomes a reflection of our creative power.
We make lasting changes.
We develop an unstoppable connection between our soul, our voice, and our life's work that inspires people into new possibilities.

When this became an embodied truth for me, I began relating to my personal and global challenges with a recognition of my power to help change them. The destructive thoughts began to disappear and I saw that we can create our reality.

This realization scared me at first. It's so much simpler, in a way, to place the responsibility for creation outside of oneself. Yet it was also comforting to come full circle and realize that the being that I was calling out for help to that night on my vision quest who responded with a wink from a hummingbird was … me. Not me here in this human body, but the divine multi-dimensional me, the Soul that transcends any physical reality. I also call this my Higher Self.

Recognizing that I AM Creatrix was not a realization I came to lightly. I think most of us wouldn't, because the idea that we are a divine being has been left out of most religions. Usually we pray to something *outside* of us.

I come to you as someone who was raised and trained within conservative and traditional systems of family, religion, education, and culture on the East Coast of the United States. With time I evolved into a renegade maverick offering radical spiritual ideas for the empowerment of women, but this wasn't a quick transition. It took decades for me to peel back the layers of conditioning.

What pulled me forward on my grand life quest to find the source of that experience I had had that night on the mountain was a knowing that lived somewhere deep in my womb that things were not as they seemed. I was taught that God existed as an entity outside of me, but this didn't ring true for me and I wasn't willing to take what I was told at face value.

As a result, I have had to sacrifice much in the name of my authenticity, sovereignty, soul purpose, and self-expression on this quest. I have navigated disapproval from my family, especially my father, who is a quintessential representative of traditional patriarchal culture. Pursuing my true path has been interpreted as a direct affront to everything he holds dear—my higher education and training (which he worked hard to provide for me), a secure, prestigious career (which I left because it was breaking me), a steady paycheck (which he sees as more important than happiness).

After decades of bending and shaping myself into the image of the good girl he would approve of, I stopped doing that. I went from being an A student, Ivy League, marketing executive for a well-known company in New York to a hippie, pagan, spiritual women's coach and DJ in San Francisco who has attended Burning Man thirteen times. This is simplifying it deliberately for effect. The nuances of my spiritual path were lost on him, which caused a lot of friction between us and we butted heads often.

For a long time I had been trying to get him to see and understand me, but I never felt that he did. Eventually my determination to make my own choices regardless of how he felt about them grew larger than my desire to keep things peaceful. I could no longer pretend to be someone else, and he could no longer tolerate that I strayed outside of the bounds of his belief systems. This came to a head when at my wedding to my second husband my father walked out.

It is not an easy thing to choose our truth and happiness over someone else's we love, but these are the choices we must make when we decide to walk our own path. Our truth can be hard-won—sometimes we emerge from this truth-diving a bit roughed up, but those battle scars are worth it because the prize is our freedom.

Not surprisingly, I have become dedicated to supporting other women who are the renegades, the pioneers, the visionaries, the rebels, the medicine women, and the way showers of all stripes—those who are trying to find a way forward off the beaten path.

You may have felt called to this book because you are hungry for the keys to your freedom. You may be here because you are committed to expressing who you truly are. Perhaps, like me, it is no longer negotiable for you—it is a soul calling. You probably recognize that you must allow yourself to evolve because you cannot create what is coming through you now from the old identity, vibration, and strategies that came from limitation. This is requiring another way of being that is untested and unfamiliar.

I know that it is not a simple choice to speak your truth and share those risky pieces of your soul that just might alienate someone. I know, and I have the battle wounds to show for it. It takes courage to change. Yet there are things ready to be birthed through you.

Events on the world stage are telling us that the time truly is now to transcend the barriers that have been in our way of realizing our highest creative visions for ourselves and the planet. It is an evolutionary imperative that more of us awaken to the truth of who we are. We need creative, generative feminine leaders who are strong enough to stand up for what they believe and share their voices, ideas, and visions.

Whether you know it or not, you, my Sister, are here as a Divine Feminine leader who can help change the face of our civilization. You are here to bring new ideas into existence. You are a fresh voice that pierces the veil of inertia that shrouds so many in our world.

It's time to turn around your lowest moments and give yourself the gift of lifting off into the life you are meant to live.

To do that, one of the most important things to understand is that you are more powerful than you have ever been told. What you can do is beyond anything you have previously allowed yourself to imagine.

It is time to clear your channel and calibrate your compass to tune to the frequency of the infinite part of you that is Creatrix.

......⚬ℐ⚬......

Deep within, there is a part of us that knows who we truly are. It is our womb knowing, that intuitive, deeply wise part of us. I believe this part of us is the Creatrix that exists within each one of us.

The Creatrix knows the breadth of her power, and she uses it to shape her reality. The Creatrix recognizes that she is a fractal of the whole and, therefore, what she does and how she chooses matters. She recognizes her own power to shift energy and the fabric of reality with her thoughts and intentions.

My decision to claim my Creatrix nature has enabled me to move through disempowering beliefs and imprints and has created different results for me in the form of an increase in happiness, financial resources, and the clarity and proliferation of my purposeful work.

If you wish this for yourself, I invite you to remember Her within you.

Here is a simple mantra that can help re-awaken Her within you:

I AM Creatrix.
I speak my reality.
The truth is what I say it is.

I AM Creatrix.
My voice magnifies, magnetizes, accelerates, awakens.
What I say resonates.

I AM Creatrix.
I create my reality.
I rise from the ashes and create anew again and again.

Reawakening the Creatrix calls for an inner revolution within each one of us. This requires us to do the work every day to choose differently. To make every choice, every thought, every action as the Creatrix.

If you moved through your life as the Creatrix, how might you do or say things differently? Would you follow others or trust yourself? Would you take the abuse or fight back? Would you stay quiet or speak up?

As the Creatrix, would you stay in the job you hate, or go get paid for the work you love? Would you choose the partner who is a decent match or the extraordinary relationship that lights you up?

There are lots of things that happen to us and a lot of events that are beyond our sphere of influence. In no way do I intend to deny the trauma we go through or insinuate that we can control everything. What we do have influence over, however, is our response to it.

We can decide that we are helpless to change our circumstances, or we can remember that we are the Creatrix and create a new experience that matches what we wish to see for our own lives and the world. It is a choice.

You are the microcosm of the macrocosm so everything that happens in your life matters and affects the fabric of your reality, which is the Universal mirror of all that is. Every interaction and every moment becomes an opportunity to express our Creatrix nature. When you do that, your life, and the world around you, can transform.

······⁙······

I invite you to begin by painting a compelling vision for your future. Then decide that this is how it will be. You can embrace your Creatrix essence and use your true creative power to bring this vision into being.

There are a lot of people living in darkness on the planet. They need us to hold the light so they can feel a glimmer of possibility and hope. When you walk through your life remembering you are the Creatrix, behaving as the Creatrix, loving as the Creatrix, you emanate that remembrance to all that come into your orbit.

When you claim the truth that you are the Creatrix of your reality, you walk forward as a sovereign being unaffected by the false beliefs, programs, and identities the world tries to put on you.

The more of us who embrace our creative power in this way, the more we can collectively change the narrative in our world.

When you are free, you free others.

When women become empowered from within, we become unstoppable forces for change.

We can harness this energy that courses through us to take a stand and decide today will be different!

Understanding this, the question then becomes:

What reality do you want to create?

ALIA (Alia Metcalf) is a renowned musical artist and women's leadership coach based in the San Francisco Bay Area. ALIA tours nationally and internationally as an original electronic music producer, vocalist, creator of the Feminine Medicine™ music project collaborating with multiple female musical artists to produce feminine-driven dance music, and a resident DJ for the global dance movement Ecstatic Dance. She is regularly featured on the stages of major festivals and conscious events. ALIA released "Feminine

Medicine Volume 1" in 2017 with a remix album and Volume 2 forthcoming. Devoted to the liberation of women around the world, ALIA is the founder of Femvolution™, the Creatrix Collective™ community, and Creatrix Academy in which she is a mentor and creative business consultant to Divine Feminine Leaders and creates training programs that support women to claim their creative power to become global influencers and luminaries. Her piece "Achieving Women's Liberation" was published in the ground-breaking book ReInhabiting the Village, *which is now the basis for a university course. A graduate of Brown University and a former corporate marketing executive for blue chip brands, ALIA has been a professional coach for more than thirteen years and a former trainer for coaching organizations including Authentic World and The Arete Experience. She is a respected feminine leader in women's entrepreneurial circles and was named a "Woman Changing the Planet" by ORIGIN magazine. She also received her MFA in Film from Academy of Art University. ALIA is an initiate of multiple mystery schools and a priestess in the 13 Moons lineage. She bridges practical approaches to manifesting our missions with esoteric wisdom combining her path as a priestess and a coach to support women in their personal empowerment. You can find information on her programs and music at **www.aliatemple.com.***

Singing Myself Awake

BY EDEN AMADORA

We have been living in a world where women have not been safe …

Have not been free to be fully expressed …

Where we have been categorized and polarized into two archetypal roles in our culture: The Whore, seen as a pleasure vehicle, and The Mother, valued and not valued as a breeder.

I know these two positions well and the cost of selling and compromising myself.

Now it is time to write a new story. That is what a "New Feminine Evolutionary" is, a writer within her own life of the new mythology of our collective story as women.

I'm writing this chapter and sharing the story of my journey and how I found a sacred third beyond these roles …

To inspire you to ask …

Beyond polarities …

What is your sacred third?

"Remember your heart girl / Remember your
intuition / Remember to recharge your batteries /
And come back / To Angelica's Kitchen."

Angelica's Kitchen

I smile flirtatiously at the cute waiter while hanging my yoga bag over the back of the seat. I love these wooden communal tables at Angelica's Kitchen, my favorite vegan spot on 2nd Avenue.

The spring sun warms my cheek as I take a few books and my new unicorn journal out of my Peruvian fabric backpack. My hand brushes the big, beautiful turkey feather from my parents' land.

London
Paris
Madrid
Barcelona
Milan
Sydney
Tokyo
NYC

...all the cities I've lived and modeled in over the past four years since graduating from high school; yet I'm on the move again, soon to be packing up my crystals and "weird little altars" as my flatmate, Sonya, calls them.

She even asked me about my painting on the wall ... the one I created from a vision of a mythical beast with the head of a lion, a body of a snake, and wings of an eagle.

"Dragons are interdimensional gate guardians," I stated, matter of factly.

I've made more money modeling than I had ever imagined, but my true passion is poetry and songwriting. I look dreamily out the window at the busy New York street beckoning the Muse to come before running off to my next casting call.

Yet, I feel the familiar pit in my stomach. Sirens wail. I can't seem to breathe deeply enough. I remember the astrologer with huge eyes who met me here a few weeks ago. This morning, he called, warning me.

"Don't go to Italy!"

"I'm the risk you take / The touch that makes
you burn / The fix you cannot break / The kiss
you must return / Your sweetest addiction /
Your sweetest affliction."

Lady of the Lake

It's hard to find macrobiotic vegan food in Milan.

I stay in, entertaining myself by meditating, practicing yoga, reading, and playing my flute. My modeling flatmates tease me; I finally succumb and go clubbing.

After all, I love dancing.

The music in the VIP room starts to move me. I feel powerful, sexy, alive … *primal.*

Lost in my own inner world, sweaty, trance-like, I open my eyes and see him standing in front of me, watching.

He's tall, dashing, square-jawed, blue-eyed, with longish tousled brown hair and a captivating smile.

"Inside desire / Am I the rider? / I turn /
I turn / I turn / Sweeter /
As I roll with this / I'm as fragile as
cigarette paper."

Turn

He hands me the long-stem red rose he just bought from the gentleman passing by our table at the fancy Italian seafood restaurant. I reach to take it, smiling … he doesn't let go.

"If you accept this, I possess you."

⋯⋯◦◦⋯⋯

His lavish, huge marble-floored apartment is full of art and antiquities. I spot peacocks and pink flamingos in the back garden.

He shows me a large room holding his prized doll collection. Lorenzo opens a glass case and toys with the doll's parasol, hat, and purse, excitedly explaining how hard it was to win her at a London auction.

He's a collector.

......⚬ℛ⚬......

Digging inside my newly gifted designer handbag—the replacement for my Peruvian backpack—I find my pack of Marlboro Lights when a tall, thin brunette model approaches me outside of the casting for Vogue Pelle.

She asks me for a cigarette, looking me up and down in assessment as all models do in this hyper competitive environment.

"Are you dating Lorenzo?"

"Yes. Why?" I retort defensively.

"Do you know he's richer than god's dog?" she challenges.

"What's that supposed to mean?"

"The devil," she says, rolling her eyes and flipping her hair as she walks away.

"You / With your anger churned lust /
With no one to trust / With your strange
appetites / You're barely alive."

Powdered Sugar

Lorenzo doesn't like my jeans and t-shirt, nor my Frye boots.

"Put on the Gucci mini dress I bought you, and heels and makeup. Hurry up!" he demands.

I open my walk-in closet full of designer clothes and go to the shelf where I'm allowed to keep my crystals and feathers; they aren't allowed in the flat … he thinks they're "creepy and disgusting." Even my chanting after yoga practice "sounds evil" and bothers him.

Holding a large quartz crystal to my heart, I breathe deeply and brush a white feather across my brow.

......ॐ......

Sitting on the terrace of the five-star hotel overlooking Lago Como, I can barely eat the gourmet meal. The meat seems too rare, too bloody.

I'm wearing the diamond bracelet he left on my pillow as compensation for his not coming home all weekend.

We made a silent deal: I stay quiet, get the lifestyle, and he takes care of me and our daughter.

It's our second bottle of Barolo. He isn't eating his osso buco: A sign Lorenzo's been on another cocaine bender.

I lift my wine glass, accidentally grazing my tender breast, still healing from the breast reduction surgery I financed from my modeling money ... without his "permission."

I wanted to restore my breasts to their original size after being talked into ridiculously large implants a year earlier, upon completing breastfeeding our daughter.

......ॐ......

An inner heat is rising, a pressure building like a weight, squeezing out my breath.

I'm suffocating, trying to keep it together like a big shaky house of cards, the flimsy facade, the pretty pretense of my life is exposed and trembling on the edge of collapse.

I'm trapped in a gilded glass cage.

I'm bought.

... And I sold myself.

Dressed and possessed.

Just like the dolls.

·····ᘒᕲᕲ·······

I want to rip off the pretty designer dress and all the diamonds I'm wearing—dropping my adornments like shackles—scream, run naked, and jump into the lake.

He looks over, scrolls down to my breasts, rolls his eyes and snarls, "You are diminished," then stares off, silently smoking his cigar.

"Chasing the one who runs / Hoping to find
me / Lost little girl inside / Circle riding /
Holding it all so tight / Who's been driving?"

Philosophy

I'm in an advanced asana—a yogic twist—at the kriya yoga ashram a couple hours outside Milan. The wiry old Indian guru asks me to lift my eye line to a precise angle, then pats his ribs strongly at his liver.

With deep compassion, he asks, "Why so disheartened and angry, little one?"

I burst into tears, choking out, "I failed my marriage!"

He makes a gesture like blowing dust off his sleeve, "Now what?"

"Coming down / I fall into shadow / In the
dark water / I learn how to paddle / Crawl /
Crawl / Crawl into my hole."

Lie in the Core

Despite the two male orderlies trying to sneak into my room, I hear rattling from the cart full of syringes and vials. They're here to take my blood while I'm sedated. The level of Haldol they gave me after not sleeping four nights in a row is still not enough to keep me knocked out.

Quickly opening my eyes, I scream, jumping up, swearing at them like a mad woman.

"Get the fuck out of my room!"

How the hell I did I get locked up in this hospital? I've lost everything that really matters, starting with my self-respect.

Eight years ago, I was confident, free, practicing Transcendental meditation daily, traveling all over the world, making tons of money.

I thought I was so damn special. Like I had indestructible wings.

That astrologer in New York warned me not to go to Italy.

He said I'd meet my polar opposite, someone who would promise me the world and take me for everything I've got.

"Flying so high with this drip inside my head /
You are my Heroin / I'm swept off my feet /
Down with the dragon again."

Heroine

BENDER

I remember …

Rubbing my eyes, head throbbing, I wake up in a tiny, unfamiliar room.

There are stains on the peeling walls. I see a large, muscular man with long, black hair and dragon tattoos covering his arms and legs. He's the Italian champion kickboxer I met in the club last night, snoring in his dingy bed.

I feel numb. The dull ache of broken heartedness is like a silent scream echoing through me. It's a deafening tone of meaninglessness.

Wanting to wash off the smell of alcohol and sex—the shame—I drag myself into the bathroom, only to find a hose and bucket full of dirty clothes.

CANCER

I remember …

The phone rings.

It's my gynecologist.

"You might want to sit down," she says.

BREAKING UP/BREAKING DOWN

I remember …

I'm split down the middle, living a totally incoherent dance of shadow and light.

The egoic grasping for validation in the seductive world of money, glamor, and fame is crashing up against all the steps I've already taken in the light of my spiritual seeking and my fragile wakefulness.

······◦৵৹······

I have the record deal. I've signed the contract. Three songs are recorded.

But I have to make amends with my record producer's wife.

They've been married twenty-two years and he's leaving her for me.

THE LANDMARK FORUM

I remember …

I speak the deepest secret for the first time: I'm here to sing Eden back on earth …

To lift the veil …

Shaking, rocking, vibrating in my seat … until I'm lifted out by some invisible force from behind.

Cracked open, I suddenly jump on stage in front of hundreds of people.

I sing.

I sing about Eden.

And true love.

… And it all starts unraveling …

SHAMANIC DEATH

I remember …

They think I'm finally sleeping.

I'm not.

I haven't for four days now.

No food or water.

My family is worried.

I don't care.

About anything.

Not my daughter. Not my record deal. Not my accolades. Not my career.

Nothing.

I'm burning in the fire.

I remember ...

Sitting in lotus position.

It's been hours looking up at my third eye.

I feel thorns piercing my skull.

I feel warm, sticky blood dripping into my eyes.

My palms are on fire.

I remember ...

Kneeling at his feet.

Sobbing.

Anointing his feet with my hair and tears.

I remember ...

I long to make love to the Beloved.

I can't find him anywhere.

I slowly bring my two hands together in union.

After desperately searching outside myself, and bizarrely projecting the Beloved on *everyone* I've encountered over the last several days, I laugh, feeling a sense of divine ecstasy as my right and left hand connect.

Tears of joy roll from my eyes.

I suddenly realize:

"Oh, it's *You!*"

"God inside / Gonna burn my fears in /
Your sweet fire
I'm gonna live / Don't need solvin'
Kill that / That kind of loving /
I'm coming in / With no one left to save now /
Can feel my phoenix rise / All bitter tears aside."

Move in Silence

Even though it looks like my life is falling apart, it can be reshaped in beauty.

I feel a peace dawning in me now, a lightness of being.

I don't need to "save" the idea of a perfect family. I don't need to "save" anyone.

........⚬ℓ⚬........

A petite, pale wisp of a Japanese woman interrupts my thoughts during our daily art therapy session in the hospital and says, "It was you!"

She smiles in a dreamy way, "It was you who was singing. I knew you would come. Thank you, angel."

> "We all have to choose / How to walk in the
> sunlight / Without fearing the dark / How
> to find faith in the future / And hold it in our
> hearts / We'll be our own saviors."

I'll Do My Best

I've just made a vow in front of my 13 Moon priestess sisters to sing for Mother—to sing for the awakening of the collective heart of humanity—and to dedicate an album to each of the 13 faces of the Goddess.

I never imagined myself as a priestess … let alone traveling an ordination path.

........⚬ℓ⚬........

I've been on a mythic heroine's journey: The descent of egoic drama; a painful tunnel; transiting through the underworld of the subconscious to transmute the darkness, to then ascend into the sunlight of a grateful, open heart and the presence that it offers.

Yet … there is no end to the ascent.

I am not "there."

I'm here to remember who I am.

That I'm already whole, already enough.

"We have received the transmission / We
have heard the mythic call / We have come
across the vast sea / In service to true love."

The Transmission

The guru in Italy told me that first I would sing like an angry woman,
then sing for yoga, and finally sing love's song like an angel.

A huge crowd is gathering in front of the stage.

I'm modeling for other performers how to bring the frequency of their
highest prayer down from the above with mudra and sacred movement.
We're grounding and preparing for the "Feminine Medicine" performance
behind the stage at the big, outdoor transformational music festival.

I put on my giant, white-feathered headdress and drop into meditation
to prepare for the opening ceremony.

It's amazing to see the audience lifting their hands together to tap into
Divine Light, raising their vibration, bringing their prayer through with the
practice I give them.

I invite them to sound the sacred sound as we "seed" the Divine Mind on
Earth together, bringing the frequency of Heaven/Eden here *now*.

"I give myself / I give myself / Permission to
live / Permission to fly."

Permission

DRAGON DREAM

I swing myself onto the saddle and grab the mane of my beast.

In place of long, white hair, my fingers wrap around long, white feathers!
We take off to the sky!

As I lean out and try to take in its neck and face, I notice fractal-like
paisley shimmers: scales, resplendent in the sunlight!

Oh my Goddess!

I am riding a giant, white dragon with opalescent scales!

I feel utter joy, extreme delight, and total freedom.

We fly fast and far with serenity and ease as the shining, dark-blue water of an ocean ripples beneath us. I marvel at the light that dances off the waves below.

My dragon swoops down, landing lightly upon a jungle path near an ancient city. She happily lays down and seems to gesture with her head that I must go on and enter this gateway alone.

I wind my way up the wild and overgrown path into the city. I see no signs of inhabitants or other large animal life, just birds and butterflies, crumbling ruins, and verdant nature, exploding flowers of every color, so lush and beautiful.

I come to a building with a large furnace-like opening on the roof. Fire shoots up and out toward the sky.

It's like a long catwalk with flames blazing from underneath through metal grates.

I see her: A black-haired, black-skinned woman standing in the flames.

She reaches out towards me, saying, without opening her mouth or making a sound, "You must come stand in the fire."

I feel a quickening inside as I move toward her but feel no fear for my life, only a sense of initiation and the potency of this request.

As I move into the heat of the flames, she dissolves before my eyes; my outstretched arm glints with a shining orange/black/gold obsidian-like glow.

I know myself to be Her.

I merge in oneness with the fire woman.

I feel an aliveness and raw, natural pleasure in my entire being. The fire purifies me, burning away all contractions, all shame, stories, and past identities that would hold me in any state less than ecstasy.

"Like a butterfly in a liquid dream /
I surrender to the miracle that's happening /
I trust and allow grace and ease /
And make a sacred vow to keep opening."

Alchemical Opening

Receiving my sword as I'm ordained, I'm challenged by my mentor to: speak truth as love; embody fierce compassion and clear presence as the Flame of Love; stand in my sovereign strength; hold myself instead of looking outside myself to be saved; and embody the balance of the sacred masculine and divine feminine as an alchemical union within.

I step forward as an ordained priestess, a focalizer of the 13 Moon Mystery School, in service to this Love.

> "I trust my knowing now / Especially in the dark / Trust my knowing now / 'Cause I know my own heart."
>
> *Trust*

I now claim this life for my own.

I rest in balance between the fire of raw passion and the unconditional embrace of the Divine Mother.

I've found my sacred third. I'm here to stand as a whole, empowered, and Sovereign being, to *model* creative love embodied.

I'm not polarized and unconsciously playing the angel/savior/mother *or* the wild/whore/primal/mad woman, but embracing both sides of my nature in balanced harmony.

I find my Heaven on Earth, the Inner Beloved, through the union of the Christ/Magdalene heart.

I'm merging with She and He through my prayer, embodiment, transmission, poem, and dream.

I am the woman
Riding the currents
Of the Dragon's song
Embodying the mystery of the
Serpent becoming the Swan.

I am a gatekeeper
Of a new dawn.

I lift my heart towards the sun
To rejoice
And receive the rays
Upon this world
To slice through the veil
For my little girl.

My life is full of initiations to keep choosing love with an open heart while breathing through discomfort to find compassion for myself and others.

The greatest gift I've received is a direct relationship to the Divine that makes this very challenging human journey feel held in an unconditionally loving embrace.

I know …

I'm awakening to hold the frequency of Eden, to be part of the unveiling that Heaven is here *now*.

"With divine intention / We're planting the seeds / Deep in our garden / Our winged hearts will sing / To be love / To see love / To bring our love here now."

Sanctuary of the Open Heart

Eden Amadora *is an archetypal channel, a mystic, and a muse. As a seeker and initiate in the mysteries from an early age, Eden remembers a direct and intimate connection with the Divine. Though her path led her into the heart of the glamor world as an international model and recording artist throughout her late teens and twenties, it was through a spiritual crisis during her Saturn Return when Eden experienced a massive kundalini awakening and turned her attention towards the inner light. After more than twenty years of yogic and shamanic training, Eden found her heart at home in the mysteries of the Sacred Feminine of the 13 Moon Mystery School. She is now an ordained priestess, a spirit, authentic voice and embodiment coach as well as a singer, ceremonialist, and prayer-formance artist. Eden's greatest joy is in witnessing the incredible transformation that occurs when she creates ceremonial space to offer women an embodied experience of working with the archetypes of the Divine feminine. She created her program "Awakening Beauty" out of her passion for helping women break free from the old paradigm of competition and comparison, and from her desire to help uplift, inspire, and support women to return to the center of their own true beauty and to fully embrace themselves as nothing less than unique and precious embodiments of the Goddess. Her clients say she is one of the most extraordinary facilitators in the arenas of archetypal embodiment and sound and movement. She is a pure presence of love and a stand for you to show up in all of your wholeness. Eden offers a safe and sacred space as a spiritual guide on this journey of awakening through 13 Moon Priestess Initiation Circles, Retreats and personal training and mentoring for women on the priestess path. Learn more:* ***www.edenamadora.com***

Feminine Evolution in Sacred Union

BY OLANA BARROS

MY EVOLUTIONARY EXPANSION

It took me nearly five decades to realize my divine perfection and innate power—embracing the freedom to be myself without apology. Just a few years ago, I was running and running and not moving forward. I served with passion and fervor, I did all the things expected of me, but there were these feelings of inadequacies and unworthiness. I felt something missing from my life. I just couldn't put my finger on it.

This is the story of my re-awakening, of my self and of my marriage.

Today's spiritual climate is calling us to rise above the old structures of partnership to create a new way to love ourselves and one another. Too many relationships have crumbled under the old structures simply because the system, the foundation, is obsolete. The worn-out patriarchal system of dominance, fear, division, dictatorship, control, and authoritative energies no longer supports the evolution of relationships. Under this influence are unhealthy patterns of superiority, manipulation, possessiveness, emotional blackmail, usury, narcissism, egoism, opportunism, blame, victimization, and competition. This has left little room for compassion, understanding, acceptance, intuition, higher wisdom, and all the missing elements that many relationships are waking up to in order to find their way into a new place of being and relating.

And that's where my story comes in, as I am coming home to my highest truth, creating more of what I desire through my life's mirrors in sacred relationships. Our relationships reflect back our perceptions of ourselves. Why not make the reflection beautiful? The soul knows the way.

EXODUS FROM THE PATRIARCHAL MATRIX

My personal journey of remembering wholeness has been catapulted by the strong patriarchal grip of religion in my life—a huge influence from my early years. Born and raised a Catholic, I've always had an infinite love for God … although I've questioned many things about religion that no leader could satisfactorily answer for me.

And so, I searched.

At thirteen, a friend introduced me to a personal relationship with Jesus. I was looking for love, acceptance, and belonging. Jesus was the cloak that covered my yearnings.

But, still, I searched.

At seventeen, I met and swiftly fell in love with the young man who ignited my soul—my husband Kaimana. It was a whirlwind that found us inseparable, pregnant, and married at eighteen years old.

That whirlwind deposited me in a family where church was a way of life. My in-laws were both ordained ministers, and we were groomed for the ministry as well. We spent the next twenty-four years serving God and our local churches in Hawaii and Nevada, amidst homeschooling and raising our four children while also working secular jobs. My husband's role as head of our household played out strongly under patriarchal influence, as was the norm for our generation.

I was accustomed to a predominantly patriarchal reign in my life through Christianity and my traditional marriage. I didn't know how to speak up for myself. I deflected my power a lot from a young age due to repetitive abuse of all forms and was silenced by many experiences that dictated authority from masculine dominance. Sexual abuse is what wounded me the most, though. I didn't even know that I had authority over my own body. It cultivated a very timid, introverted, broken girl. It took me years to heal this deep-rooted wound through forgiveness.

I served as Women's Leader in several churches, and over the course of two decades, my ministry to women was my most beloved yet challenging path of service. I encountered many wounded women from all walks of life, of all ages, too numerous to count. This work taught me so much about our feminine disempowerment, which also revealed how oppressed we've been for centuries. That began to make more sense as I was guided by Divine Mother to see through new lenses.

Kaimana and I served and served as spiritual leaders and as mentors, and we began to experience burnout. It became apparent to us that we were no longer serving from passion but from responsibility and obligation. We found ourselves slowly questioning our foundational beliefs as Christians and our positions as leaders that were responsible for so many souls. We were both stirred with many questions that grew stronger. We wanted to create a bridge out of religion somehow.

Our spiritual awakening was catapulted by our feelings of misalignment with our shifting ideals and new awareness of consciousness and spirituality. Our roles as pastors evolved quickly as our views of dogma and religion caused us to question every belief we had adopted from early childhood into adulthood. It was subtle at first, but then as our inner voices guided our questioning everything, we eventually found ourselves in a life we no longer resonated with.

We slowly began to share our evolving perspectives on our expanding spiritual views with our fellowship group, and the more we outgrew our old beliefs the more we wanted to leave our pastoral positions. It was a difficult decision, as it affected so many people we have loved and served alongside for years.

Leaving didn't come easy, as my husband felt a very strong sense of responsibility to the church we co-founded. It was his visionary insight to create a place that gave people permission to cross over the bridge of religious conformity into spiritual sovereignty. It took him getting very ill with extreme adrenal fatigue syndrome—causing his body to slowly shut down, which brought him close to dying—before we actually left our church. He was taken to the emergency unit at our local hospital due to symptoms that resembled a stroke or heart attack, and in that moment he was unaware of all personal information.

Two weeks later we stepped down from our positions completely. And honestly, it would be much easier to say that we came out of the church relieved. We didn't. We were wrought with heartbreaking pain from leaving and too many other feelings to articulate. But we had no choice—it was as if our souls took us out in order to evolve from the place we were stuck in.

Our evolution wasn't easy, and it caused quite a rumbling in our community, to say the very least. Long-term relationships began to crumble and people in our community began to hear of our exit from the church. Some snubbed us, but others embraced us.

One of the most painful things I had experienced within the church was the energetic masculine challenging me in the form of sisterhood with co-leaders. As I found my truth emerging, I shared my emerging path of feminine freedom in conversations and talks. I was severely rejected and was told to be silent about my newfound freedom and found myself being put in my place by peers. Even though it was empowering to some women in our fellowship group, it was also threatening to our co-leaders because we were changing swiftly. I encountered resistance and strong, fear-based judgment by the women in our leadership team. My husband did as well.

We were all strong men and women serving together. But the more I spoke of freedom from dogma, the more resistance I faced. My husband didn't have the backlash quite like I did. So I held my voice back for a short time until we left.

MY AWAKENED FEMININE VOICE

Eventually I found my true voice. It came out initially as anger, rage, intolerance, rebellion, and resistance to any authority or anything trying to silence me. It had been suppressed for so long that being free from religious restraints was the impetus that surged within me to want to share it. I found an inner rage that needed a pathway to be released, expressed, and defined. As I've healed the ancient feminine wound within, I've also released my anger and resentment towards the patriarchal system. In doing so, I've been able to feel more attuned to my feminine wild power.

It was my initiation into the dark night of the soul that provoked the need to go within and disengage from all outside influences. This truly opened me up to a higher consciousness, connecting me to my truth, to what truly matters to my soul and especially to using my voice.

Feeling relieved of all leadership responsibilities gave me the freedom to explore the very strong desire to connect with Divine Mother, the Divine Feminine, and all that was becoming so much more resonant for me. She wooed me deeper within and my life began to take on a new path of meaning and purpose.

When my wild woman of sensuality and freedom in my sexuality emerged, it felt so sacrilegious at first. I had denied my inner wild for so long that it felt like sinful indulgence. But I followed my inner longing, and it felt so right. Ironically, it felt pure and holy. I felt uncaged and loosened from shackles that kept female energy bound for centuries. I knew it was collective, as I experienced it so deeply and individually.

I'm drawn to all things that nurture my feminine roar. I found women in sacred circles that speak about ritual, ceremony, and devotion as High Priestess, as a vessel for the Goddess. This rocked my world. As I allowed myself to connect to my sacred truth, I have deep remembrance of being a sacred High Priestess and other roles as well that served in great devotion to Divine Mother and all the many Feminine practices. It's been an intuitive journey of becoming more soulfully aligned.

HEALING THE DIVINE MASCULINE WITHIN

In the healing of the feminine and masculine energies within me, my Beloved Kaimana intuitively allowed healing within himself, too. It happened naturally as the rising of the feminine energy in us both began to allow a more loving and compassionate space for the masculine to rise also to be healed. It's been a very sacred time for my husband and I to be vulnerably open, transparently honest, and fully seen, naked, and unashamed with one another. The raw wounds from the patriarchal rule has affected us all, so this healing has been essential in our wholeness unfolding.

We were both molded with such a strong influence of structure in controlling leadership and dogma that we had to break out of the mold that had shaped us so intently for decades. Kaimana had denied his innermost feelings of sexual desires for years, feeling shameful for such innate and natural feelings. I, too, had so much to unearth due to sexual abuse and trauma from a young age. Together, we've been able to free ourselves from the rigid structures and explore new definitions of what has been so exhilarating and expansive for us both through loving and honoring one another deeply and completely.

The Divine Masculine energy has been given a sacred place to heal in other ways within our union as much as the Divine Feminine. Kaimana and I have been able to explore and co-create a new definition for sacred marriage. Sacred marriage may look different for each couple seeking this path. For us, the dreams and desires we both hold within have developed a new meaning of sovereign partnership. We were both so accustomed to our traditional marriage, doing many things together as a couple including our family, especially in the ministry, that now we're allowing space to explore what lights us up individually.

By connecting within to our higher selves, we are able to see one another without filters, letting go of all past experiences and patterns that have dictated to our parameters or constructs of relationships. To be able to see one another from the higher self allows for relationships to experience higher frequencies of exchange where you and your partner engage from a higher perspective. This creates an open, expansive field for your relationship to interface with another, to allow for divine love, freedom, and your true nature as a divine being to be fully expressed.

The old structures of expectations and responsibilities have shifted into fresher agreements and commitment to our highest and best good as creators of our desired lives. It has been serving us both very well in this new flow of sacred partnership, and we're continually expanding and growing more free in our love and devotion to this higher way of loving ourselves and one another.

SACRED PARTNERSHIP

As my beloved and I are learning to navigate our higher consciousness and new ways of being with one another, we've created the unspoken language of sacred space and extra grace within our relationship. By simply allowing it to be our core agreement for ourselves and one another when we feel challenged or out of sorts, this creates a safe and loving place for us to grow, expand, and express what feels natural and, sometimes, even edgy.

We've moved through so much inner healing for such a long season that grace and love have become a powerful way for us both to navigate transformative changes. One of our agreements is to see one another in our highest while being unattached to expectations of how we each choose to express our higher selves in daily life.

I chose to forgive my husband for his participation in the collective patriarchal role he played of being dominant, authoritative, and even abusive in our younger years. He chose to forgive me for being a nagging and ball-busting wife conditioned with patterns that taught me to fight and manipulate—the only way I knew to get what I needed and wanted.

One of our more recent shifts was his attachment to my role as his wife—he's been accustomed to my serving him, cooking for him, doing the domestic duties and still contributing financially to our household. He's also been attached to his role as a man. He carries his responsibilities as provider and protector very seriously and at times has overwhelmed himself in carrying so much of this burden. When he's caught up in this place, I remind him to share the load of financial responsibilities. I show him support in ways that I know will help him shift his energies, enabling him to find his center once again.

Although he sees us as divine partners, our daily roles are still expanding and the lines are becoming less structured and more in conscious partnership.

If you are as blessed as I am to have a divine partner daring to stand by your side when walking through the darkest night of the soul, even daring to push your edges of familiar structures, you'll understand what I mean when I speak of sacred partnership. While it isn't necessary for your own wholeness to occur, it is in my experience that a sacred partnership creates a holy foundation of unconditional love, support, and safety for you both to cultivate expansion as you navigate ascension together.

In this sacred space of love and grace, our shadow parts can come forth safely without fear of being rejected, judged, or abandoned. This is so necessary for both of us when walking through our dark caverns and embracing our shadow selves as well. In embracing the shadow parts we make way for the portal of our brilliant light to shine through.

This has played out in our relationship when I've felt insecure and unsure of our evolving marriage, especially as we keep expanding within ourselves—he doesn't patronize me by saying what he thinks I want or need to hear from him. Instead of judging me, he invites me back into my truth, asking, "What do you desire to experience in our relationship? Do you want to create us falling out of love, or do you want to create us continuing to grow deeper in our love?" Rather than feeling judged, I feel empowered and I center myself in my truth again.

What we've learned over years of habitual patterns is that we're on a journey of growth and expansion into our truth as we partner together in co-creating powerfully what we both truly desire while allowing space and grace to carry us through changes.

This sacred incubation within the chalice of divine love that we've co-created is the perfect place for the fire of purification to purge all that no longer serves our highest purpose. This is when divine union beautifully unfolds.

The profound part of this experience is that our souls know when it's my turn or my Beloved's turn to be the one receiving and giving support. The wisdom of our soul guides our spiritual maturity. Our part is to continue to trust our soul's wisdom deeply as well as one another's, to know without hesitation that Kaimana has my highest and best interest in his intention and I for him as well.

In this place of safety, we can let go of labels, attachments, judgments, old patterns, and filters to make way for a higher vision of love to be created. When we shift out of fear and more into divine love, we co-create a model of loving unity and balanced energies within the container of sacred and loving relationships.

This is the way we've been designed to be.

Olana   Barros   is   an ordained minister, clairvoy- ant oracle and seer, evolu- tionary author, speaker, and feminine leader for the 21st century Divine Feminine rising. She is wife to her beloved husband Kaimana for over thirty years and mother to their four amaz- ing children, ages 13, 22, 25 and 30. Olana offers her powerfully transformational
program, The Multidimensional Women's Leadership, a 13-month immersion experience of feminine principles with a cutting-edge mentorship program that sets women on course for global legacy and leadership, which also includes a retreat in Hawaii. With her twenty-five years of seasoned spiritual leadership, Olana facilitates women through deep transformational breakthroughs as they awaken to their divine feminine wholeness, embody their multidimensional expressions, and unleash their creative power to intentionally design the life of global leadership they are meant for. Olana and her Twin Flame love Kaimana are the co-creators and facilitators of Soul-to-Soul Sacred Union Immersion, which is a relationship-transforming experience for five days and five nights in Hawaii, where they support Twin Flame Unions and Conscious Couples who desire to transcend all relationship challenges and attune to their Divine Love, sacred connection, and deepened, lasting intimacy, all for the higher purpose of their unified mission as their soul's calling together. Her passion is to facilitate transformation by speaking, writing, teaching, and mentoring women through retreats and programs in which the client embodies her mul- tidimensional essence. Olana's core message empowers women to deepen into self-love, embodied truth, and great trust in their innate wisdom and intuition. She pioneers a new breed of womanhood that is in a loving, sacred relationship all while embodying her sovereign truth and feminine wisdom through divine partnership in a Twin Flame union. Learn more: **OlanaBarros.com**

On the Wings of Acceptance

BY REBECCA CAVENDER

A wild bird flies

whole earth
in rapturous wonder:

Old ways die.

I want him off me.
I can't breathe.
I look up.
He's much bigger, much older.
The pressure hurts.
"Shhhh."
"That's a good girl."

My body goes cold.
I'm not here.

He's supposed to be our friend.
… I shiver.

He tastes his fingers.
Smiles.
"Good little princess."

......ଚ୨ଚ......

Beloved child of light,
daughter of the One Heart,
I wrap my arms around your
divine innocence,
the spark of life that navigates your wonder,
your soft spirit.

You are forever adorned
in the beauty of
true love,
the love of blissful freedom.

......ଚ୨ଚ......

I won't tell.
I'll forget.
I'll pretend this never happened.

My long hair is cut short.
I can't cover my face with it anymore.
Frozen on the stairway.
Embarrassed.
Exposed.
I don't want them to see me.

The sky is dark.
Night passes quickly through the rear window of the car.
Stars encircle, follow.
They draw me in, a vortex of vast emptiness,
a cosmos of possibility.
It's clear:
I don't belong here.

Don't they see I'm hiding?

Follow that star,
your True North,
the design of your heart
ignited
seeking
the virtue of your soul.
It is here.

My neck stiffens, aches.
I try taking deep breaths to open, feel, stop restricting.

No matter how I bend, no matter how I
push,
press,
please
… it's not enough.
It's not enough to make me feel loved, seen, heard … safe.

Yet there is a piano.
And a pen.
My notebook.
The wildflowers and clay mud.
Hay and daffodils.

Come to the forest,
Hear my call.
The wind whispers my eternal name.
Find me in the oak moss, sweet child,
the drifting stream.
Let the waters carry you home.

The woods are my sanctuary, my inner world.
I follow the long grass to the creek, talk to the oaks.
The wind calls back, beckoning me.
I'll write the stories I hear.

Upon my horse, I'll sing the ancient one's songs, let the
cool breeze carry them to unknown lands: nymphs, fairies, witches.
I travel there in my wanderings,
follow the sound,
make friends with cows and honeysuckle and
save the bees.

When the fog settles in after rain,
I'll dig for arrowheads
under slippery roots.

······⚬⟑⚬······

I am your sanctuary.
Your eventide.

······⚬⟑⚬······

Magic surrounds me, takes me in:
My escape, my respite, my peace …

… from a family split down the middle,
a sharp axe breaking a branch,
crushed like a rotting apple.
I cower, hide in my room.
Then:

Create a new whirlwind.
Command equity,
stand upon my bed,
young, demanding,

in booming voice,
without fear,
explicit in my duty:
To protect, to safeguard.

Next time, though, I run.
Get pulled.
Slapped shut.
Next time,
I stay quiet.

......⁊ℭ......

Beloved girl of magic,
I am always with you.
Call on me through the portals of your
childhood walls.
I'll arrive when you ask.
I'm there when you don't.

Beloved girl of magic,
take the fearsome cracks,
the raging stones,
and make a story-song.

......⁊ℭ......

I don't believe them anymore.
It's a betrayal.
It feels like lies: twisted use of power, manipulated to hold us down.

(I'm tired of being held down.)

The clarity of inequity spits in my face: You're not a man. You can't bless.
Your touch is sinful.

They say: We hold the priesthood, the sacrament, the sanctity.
They say: We weave the way the truth is told.

I want to know about Heavenly Mother.
I want to know *Her.*

They say: You can pray for guidance if you want ... but you know what the answer will be.

So:
Be a righteous daughter of God.
Repent.
Cover your arms.
Pull down your skirt.
Pull up your shirt.
Close your legs.
Straighten your morals.

······◦⌘◦······

I am the One temple of everlasting light.
I am the heart of union,
the electric fire.
There is nothing to seek.
There is nothing to know.
I am the One temple of everlasting light.

······◦⌘◦······

I'm not worthy of the temple?
God is quiet.
My chalice is poison.

Open your eyes, dear one.
Feel my gaze upon your saddened face.
There is no mistake.
There is no perfection.
Open your ears, dear one.
Open your ears!

I won't be held down.
I won't be silenced.
Not by *you*.

Only *I* have that power.
Only *I* am allowed to silence myself.
An act of human disobedience: Self-dismemberment.
The choice to detach.
Disintegrate.
Disappear.

You disapprove?
I'm not enough?
I'll leave:
Take this last breath into everlasting sleep.
(I don't want to be here, anyway.)

I cup your wet cheeks in the palms of my hands,
sweet girl.
Do you feel me surround you,
breathing life back into you?

I gift you choice.

What will you choose?
What will you see?

On the day the crocus bloomed, snow fell.
It kissed the petals of courage,
the courage to survive winter.
I cry.
Kneel.
Choose life.

Cherry blossoms erupted like an electrical storm
or lightning caught on a summer horizon,
bright with grace, renewal.
I promise to look in others' eyes.
I promise to see them, feel them.
I promise to witness pain behind a well-practiced grin.

The thing about lightning is there's intensity:
Bolts of rarefied currents, surging through your body.

How do I contain this?

My large shape doesn't grant societal permission for an erotic,
fully expressed life.
My large shape betrays me as I cloak her with a pretty face.
My large shape says: *Stop. Enter only if you dare.*

Enter your holy temple.
Open the doors to your ecstatic essence.
Surrender to the sacred currents of poetry,
pulsing through your vessel.
You are the holy temple.

This body isn't mine.
It contorts.
Swells.
Contracts.
Undulates in weight, movement, sound.
It holds me down.
Keeps me apart.

He says it
—*my body*—
is too much.
Not enough.
Unacceptable.
He could've done better.
Found someone slimmer.
More exotic.
Darker hair.
Smaller stomach.
He says he'll leave.
Start over.
Untethered.
Un-*familied.*

I know how to do this:
Withdraw.
Withhold.

Observe quietly ... wait for the finale, the last straw:
Another letter.
Another talk.
Another cup of tea to announce his unhappiness.
A divorce.

I'll wait, enveloped in a smile ... polite.

Nice girl, emotionally absent girl, kind-eyes girl:
I just won't make you dinner, as you requested.

I'll stop asking about your day.
I'll turn away from you in bed.
I'll encourage you to stay away from home—
with your friends (with her)—it doesn't matter.
Long-suffering patience earns me kudos and feeds my inner martyr.
I've silently been at this game of hide and seek since I was a little girl.
Oh, yes: I know how to do this.

······⌾⌾······

Intimacy.
Intimacy.
Intimacy.
What will you let in?
Who will you see?
How will you love?

······⌾⌾······

When will it change?
Will I stop holding back my truth?
Will I anchor myself in the space between the breath before breath?
Will I disrobe—reveal—myself?

I swallow my words, dark and whole.
I choke on false strength and old fear.
Unworthiness rears its head in the formlessness
of ghosting
and the overwhelming,
silent ache
to be seen (and not seen!).

I swing on the paradoxical pendulum in search of my truth, my gnosis,
my path.

......⚬⧜⚬......

My dear woman,
Your path is told along the lines of your palms,
Your starburst third eye,
the venus rose in your heart,
the diamond on your fire tongue.

Trace your ecstasy across words of light,
the sound of love.

Let them welcome you home.

......⚬⧜⚬......

In the etching of my bones, I yearn for my
peacefully electrifying home.

A storm is rolling in. The horizon gives it away.
Elephant grass sways and the scent of wet on cracked land
intoxicates me.
The Masai Mara spreads ahead;
wind plays in my hair.
Lions, too, lift their heads, manes flowing,
embodiment of presence.
Sitting atop the Land Rover, I spread my arms,
welcome the wild,
make love to the earth, the rapturous sky;
Ah, how the elements consume me.

Most leave the waters in a good storm.
It's then I enter.
Primal ocean licking my bare skin,
the cool rain kisses my mouth.
Gasping, I'm in love with the contrast of
dense clouds, erupting sun.
It's the orgasmic poetry of life.

......ᛜ......

My breath surges through you,
the sensual touch,
the gasp of truth.
I live in the tips of your fingers,
within the center of your heart.
Remember me.
Remember you.
Remember us.

......ᛜ......

Back slices.
The burning heat escalates.
A tight spine storing old memories.

I wonder if I'm back to half-truths again … compromising, pacifying,
misaligned.

"Just put your head down," I whisper to myself.
"Keep your mouth shut," I groan.
"Stay still," I plead with my body.

I want to push through the imprint of being cast out.
Not enough/too much.

......ᛜ......

There is only belonging in my womb of knowing.
There is only explosion of acceptance.
Burn in this with me.

......ᛜ......

She places her hands on me.
Light touch here: And a reverberation of ancient patterns sear/seer through.
Light touch there: And a stabbing pain permeates my cells.
I cry, release.
Sound the anguish of untold stories ...
The collective-personal tales of mistrust and abuse ...
the repeated messages of:

Do as you're told.
Be a good girl.
Hide.
You're not safe.
You don't belong here.
You do NOT get to choose.

The phoenix catches my attention in the mirror.
She spreads herself across my right shoulder in honor of my foremothers.
My mother, aunts, grandmothers across the lineages were pushed down,
sacrificed,
took their unhappiness.
... And they rose above the decay around them,
with soft strength,
taking wing to their own path.

I'm here to claim their gift.
To reconcile the wound.

I feel the gentle call of the wind from my childhood as she breathes outside,
playing in the chimes, sounding music within me.

My diamond-eyed phoenix tattoo stares,
confronts:
Will I trust my desires, my vision, my inner knowing?
Will I *really* show up?

·······♾········

My dear,
Climb upon my back,
feel the beat of my heart in your starry womb.
I am your crystalline essence,
your mandala of golden light,
dripping in honey-kisses.
I am born of the cosmic sea,
erupting in erotic union
at the soles of your diamond feet.

·······♾········

Truth is: I don't do it the conventional way.
Never have.
My journeys diverge,
      bend;
sometimes
            stray.

Eventually, there is a union of complementary nuanced differences,
bowing to the sacredness of it all.

I feel divine presence in a succulent peony and
taste it on the lips of a beautiful man
eager,
open.

I'm remembering to presence this divinity in my body.
I'm remembering to accept the wings of my full being.

There is a humility in the grand nothingness and the infinite everything.
I want to merge between them.
The truth that lights my being echoes:

Listen.
Just listen.
And follow your truth.

······ঙ৪৹······

I anoint your graceful union,
Your starlight wisdom,
the truth of sacred home.

Lay your head across my vast sky,
as I penetrate your depth of heart.

You are the Beloved of My Beloved:
My Beloved, Your Beloved,
One.

······ঙ৪৹······

My fingertips tell a story of love.
They touch skin, pen, anointing a new myth.
It's time to write stories into hearts,
write desires into ashes,
blow them through the rising heat,
the unearthed beginning;
bless them with the oil of ecstatic poetry …
Travel their wild song.

The drum enters my soul,
resounds across the curved meadow of my body.
It carries me from safe forest to heavenly infinity:
a rapturous glen, an electric field.
The wholeness vibrates a respiration,
a unique code of light—symbols of night—
its luminescence untamed innocence

and fierce vibrance.
A star-story written on the ethers.

I'm here now: Rebecca.
Throat open: I sound our medicine.
Fingers spread: I write our truth.

I follow the temple of my heart.
In gratitude, offering open hands to
All The Ways
that dance in harmony.

......∘ℒ∘......

We are here:
Palms up.
Opalescent sword of truth within your heart,
a golden crown of grace.
Embodiment of ousia,
your true destination,
eternal divine spark.
The winged one returns:
Layla of the Starry Night.

......∘ℒ∘......

Rebecca Cavender is a best-selling author, poet, and professional writer living in one of the beautiful valleys in Washington State. In a uniquely catalyzing and lyrical voice, Rebecca intuitively scribes words that serve as medicine so you may feel deeply seen and heard. She provides a variety of intuitive writing services: Divine Feminine copywriting and editing for soulful entrepreneurs; book editing and coaching; sacred writing circles/ workshops; scribed oracle readings and written blessings. As a certified  "Scent Priestess," she also offers in-person anointings. When she's not writing, you can find her deepening in the priestess path, being with her amazing daughter, or hanging out at one of the many Pacific Northwest coffee joints. Learn more: **www.rebeccacavender.com**

Lighting the Torch of Truth

BY ALLISON CONTE

Great Mystery,
teach me how to trust
my heart,
my mind,
my intuition,
my inner knowing,
the senses of my body,
the blessings of my spirit.
Teach me to trust these things
so that I may enter my Sacred Space
and love beyond my fear,
and thus Walk in Balance
with the passing of each glorious Sun.

~Lakota Prayer

Dear sister, as I write this, my heart is as bright as the morning sun that is shining over a vast expanse of Colorado blue sky, snowy mountain peaks, and lush forests. I'm spending a week on solo retreat so I can unplug from noise of the outside world and tune into the quiet knowing inside me.

Peace and quiet is important not only for the writing process but also for the content, because I'm here to write about why this inner voice matters and why you must trust yours.

Despite having a clear intent, a clear calendar, and a clear space in which to work, however, I began the retreat in a decidedly *unclear* state of mind … doing the very thing I am hoping to teach you *not* to do: questioning my intuition.

My old friend Doubt had a good time messing with me. Suddenly, I didn't know anything: *Is this the right topic? Who am I to write about it? Will anyone be interested?*

This familiar bout with doubt also happened the first time I gave a public talk about trusting intuition. That morning, my news feed presented an article about a woman who had not trusted her intuition. As a result, she almost got herself killed on a date with a dangerous man.

And *BAM.* In a flash, I knew I was on the right track.

Sister, if you remember only one thing from this chapter, remember this: You must learn to hear, and trust, your intuition. Something much bigger than a writing project is at stake here. What's at stake could be your whole life, and possibly all human life.

More on this later … But first, a story:

Many years ago, I had my own experience of getting involved with the wrong man. I was seventeen when I met my first husband, and my youthful gullibility was a good match for his insecurity-masked-as-confidence. On our first date, he lied to me. It was a big lie: about who he was, where he worked, and what he did for a living. When I discovered this, my intuition alarm went off: *Warning! Warning! Don't trust a man who lies on the first date!*

And you know what I did? I hit the over-ride button. I silenced that inner voice. Instead of trusting myself, I trusted him. I gave him a pass.

As you can imagine, it was an awful marriage. He became abusive and was unemployed for many years. I brought home the bacon, raised the children, and tried to smile. Meanwhile, like a frog boiling in hot water, my soul was slowly dying.

Why did I put up with this for so long? Because I didn't trust myself to know when it was time to end the relationship. Even when he crossed the line into physical abuse—in front of our two small children—still, I doubted myself. It took me over a year know for sure.

This story does not end well.

When I finally filed for divorce, he imploded, alternating between rage and depression. He refused to move out of the house while he dragged out the divorce proceedings for more than two years. He spent what was left of our savings (most of which was drained from his years of unemployment) to buy a house, then put his mother's name on it so it could not be claimed as a shared asset.

But none of that hurt as much as this: He convinced our little boys that the divorce was all Mommy's fault, that I was an irresponsible mother, and worst of all, that I didn't care about them.

I learned the hard way that not trusting myself could destroy lives.

Sister, have you ever pushed the over-ride button on your intuition? Have you given a pass to something or someone that you knew was not good for you? Or perhaps you knew at first, but then you doubted what you knew … You didn't trust yourself.

We cannot afford to do this anymore—not in our personal lives, not at work, and not as citizens.

In the United States, we are inundated with fake news, "alternative facts," and constant lies from the highest ranks of government. In this post-truth world,[1] the president speaks the truth only 5 percent of the time[2]—and still gets a pass from millions of people.

> "The future of America, indeed the future
> of the world, depends on brave, thoughtful
> people like you insisting on truth and
> integrity right now, every day."
>
> ~Hillary Clinton

This, dear one, is called *gas-lighting*. A term that arose from a 1938 film, gas-lighting refers to a situation in which false information is presented in a way that *makes the receiver doubt their own memory, perception, or sanity.*

This story will not end well.

As the patriarchy thrashes around in its death-throes, it will become more dangerous than ever. Things will get worse before they get better. We will need our wits and our power. We must be able to see in the Darkness. We've got to be able trust our memory, perception, and sanity.

In other words, we must be connected to our gift of Feminine wisdom: intuition.

When we are seated in sovereignty and connected to inner knowing, we are unlikely to be fooled by the manipulations and false narratives of others. We will be able to lead the way for others through the Darkness toward the Light, because we can clearly see the path ahead.

UNWRAPPING THE GIFT

It's easy to see this gas-lighting as a disaster with no upside, and grasp at solutions touted by talking heads on the nightly news: Buy a subscription to the *New York Times*! Read up on climate change science! Double-down on fact-checking!

But while those solutions may be necessary, they're not sufficient. As Feminine evolutionaries, we must look beyond the obvious.

The Feminine path takes us down and in to the heart of Darkness, where we discover the Light that was present in it, all along. The Dark Goddess is asking us to journey to the Underworld, where we can see this gas-lighting situation for what it really is: *a gift.*

This notion of shadow[3]-as-gift comes from Shamanism, the world's oldest wisdom tradition. Shamanism teaches us to find the gift of the shadow by turning it sideways, upside down, or inside out, to reveal a deeper truth … alchemizing lead into gold.

What could possibly be the gift in gas-lighting? Here's what I see:

Shadow (lead)	Deeper Truth (gold)
We are drowning in a sea of "alternative facts"	We must learn to swim in Non-Ordinary Reality[4]
We cannot trust external authorities with the truth	We must learn to trust the truth of our inner authority (intuition)

Looking at it this way, we can see this gas-lighting situation for what it is: a nudge from the Universe to help humanity evolve. And we do need to evolve! For Goddess' sake, we will either evolve or go extinct.

Here's the evolutionary story:

We have reached the limits of scientific-materialism. As humans are prone to do, we've taken a good thing and gone too far with it. We've outsourced the truth to external sources and lost touch with the internal source. We've glorified reason and atrophied intuition. We abandoned magic in favor of logic. We threw the baby out with the bathwater and called it superstition.

> "The intuitive mind is a sacred gift and the rational mind is a faithful servant. We have created a society that honors the servant and has forgotten the gift."
>
> *~Albert Einstein*

To evolve, we must include and transcend the modern era's obsession with reason. We need an upgrade, a new level of human understanding, a new form of intelligence. To take us into the future, we need "integrated intelligence"—which combines the reason (a Masculine capacity) and intuition (a Feminine capacity).[5]

As a leadership coach, I see a future in which the best leaders will blend the best of both worlds: They will make decisions based on information from the physical realm and the intuitive (non-physical) realm. They will read spreadsheets and energy signatures. They will consult the board of directors and the Council of Light. They will hire strategists and psychics. Their skills will include management and magik.

CLEARING THE PATH FORWARD

How will we get there? We'll need to rebuild the atrophied muscles of intuition and learn new skills (see tips at the end of this chapter). But that's just the beginning.

We've got deeper work to do.

We need to move some obstacles out of the way. You can be smart, accomplished and confident and still have internal blocks to accessing and trusting your intuition. So if you want intuition to be a trusted advisor, clearing these blocks is paramount.

We block intuition in three ways: Dismissal, Doubt, and Over-Ride.

Dismissal

Dismissal happens in a flash. Because intuitive hits are very subtle and lightning-fast, they are easy to miss. As soon as the information comes in, you immediately dismiss it as meaningless: *That's just random; it doesn't mean anything.* Dismissal happens so quickly, you probably don't realize that you've done it until perhaps sometime later, when you realize that the flash of intuition was correct.

Soon after my husband and I moved into our mountain house, I awoke one night and sat straight up. I "knew" that a bear had come through the window into the house. Since I didn't hear anything with my physical ears or see anything with my physical eyes, I dismissed this thought as ridiculous and went back to sleep.

The following day, my next-door neighbor came over to tell me that a bear had broken into his kitchen. My intuitive GPS had been off by a few yards—but still, it was *right* (and my accuracy has improved since then!). If I had acted on this intuition, I might have been able to save the bear; instead, he was chased off with a stun gun and eventually captured by wildlife rangers.

Doubt

Doubt takes a bit longer than dismissal. You might see or know something very clearly, and then Doubt comes in and begins to erode your knowing, over time. This is like building a sand castle and then watching the waves slowly wash it away.

A few years ago, I had a vision that a great Darkness would come to humanity. My spirit guides informed me that I was meant to share this information with those who had ears to hear. But instead, I listened to the voice of Doubt: *Did I really see that? Who am I to know? Will I scare people? Will I lose credibility? Will they kill me?* So I didn't share it.

Now, with Donald Trump in the White House, American democracy under threat, and North Korea's missiles within striking distance of the United States, I can see that the Darkness from my vision is gathering in strength.

And yet, my first reaction to Trump's election was disbelief: *How did I not see this coming?* But the truth is, I did see it coming. I saw it ... then doubted it.

Over-ride

With over-ride, it's obvious that you know what you know, but you choose not to listen or take action.

A girlfriend of mine, who is leading a project to save a large swath of rainforest in Central America, was approached by a lawyer from New York City, who said he would help with the legal contracts. He offered to sign a robust non-disclosure agreement (NDA), which requires him to keep confidential any sensitive information about the project.

When the deal was at its peak phase, however, he changed his tune: He told her he would bring in the perfect investors—if she would release him from the NDA.

"I should have listened to my intuition," she said. "I knew something felt 'off' about this man, but I over-rode my knowing because I needed his help. I gave my power over to him." Thankfully, my friend did not give him the power he was seeking, but the project fell several months behind as she figured out how to work around him.

> REFLECTION: *Can you think of examples from your own life when you dismissed, doubted, or over-rode your inner knowing? What were the consequences?*

GOING DEEPER

If you find yourself dismissing, doubting, or over-riding, you're not alone. Most of us don't trust intuition.

Why not? Lots of reasons:

Rational scientific materialism

As children, we are taught to ignore our subtle senses and value only what we can perceive with our physical eyes, ears and hands. Instead of being taught to dream and create, many of us were required to memorize information rather than thinking and intuiting for ourselves. Most schools do not effectively teach the creative process or the scientific method (which if used well, actually does include intuition).

Collective trauma and soul-wounds

During the European Inquisition and later during the Salem witch trials, thousands of people (mostly women) with intuitive gifts were killed for using them. These killings are deeply engrained in our collective psyche.

Fear of overwhelm

Because empaths and intuitives are sensitive to input from the unseen realm, we often try to avoid overwhelm by installing energetic "blinders" or other protective mechanisms.

Past-life experiences

If you don't believe in past lives, no worries; there's plenty of work to be done on your childhood patterns from this lifetime (we'll get to that next). If you do believe that past lives could be affecting your intuitive abilities, it's a good idea to clear any past lives that are negatively affecting you now. If you've never done this, it's a good idea to seek professional help.

Childhood experiences

Your childhood experiences hold the primary key to clearing blocks around intuition. The good news is that it's possible to clear these blocks!

My own intuitive block started at around age four, when my parents gas-lighted me. They lied about my mother's mental health (she was chronically depressed) and about the state of their marriage (they were chronically disconnected).

Although their intentions were benevolent—they were trying to protect me—I was forced to choose between what I perceived and what they told me. As children do in order to survive, I believed my caregivers. It was safer to trust the external authorities than to trust my inner authority. But this seriously damaged my inner compass.

Not only did my parents lie to me but I also lied to myself. I gas-lighted myself. I developed a core belief that said, *I can't see what's happening. I can't trust what I perceive.*

Lies create static in the subtle energy field, blocking intuitive signals from getting through. So I had static both outside (from my parents) and inside (from myself).

When I was a teenager, my parents announced that they were getting a divorce. A year later, my mother attempted suicide. I was devastated because I hadn't seen either of these things coming. I was actually more upset about being blindsided than I was about the possibility of losing my mother!

This experience reinforced my internalized beliefs: *I can't see what's happening. I can't trust what I perceive.*

For two decades afterward, I lost access to intuition. My inner reading screen was offline.

We all have childhood wounds around which we construct core beliefs and coping strategies; these are designed to keep us safe and connected to love (even if it's a painful love). Later in life, these strategies become dysfunctional and stand in the way of what we really want.

The key to releasing these blocks is not to destroy or disavow them but to gently uncover them, offering love and gratitude for their service. This way, we can dissolve the blocks and replace them with a more functional system of protection.

REFLECTION: *In what ways have you blocked your inner knowing? Looking deeper, can you see what might have been the source(s) of this mistrust?*

STEPPING THROUGH THE PORTAL

My intuition came back online when I began to heal the trauma wounds from my past lives and childhood traumas. In recent years, this inner knowing has steered me toward blessings and away from bad situations more times than I can count.

For example, let's return to the theme of dangerous men: A certain spiritual teacher was once very popular in my community. The first time I saw him on stage at a conference, however, my body revolted. I didn't know why, but by this point, I had learned to trust my body signals … so I stayed out of the room. At a second conference, a friend attempted to introduce me to him, but I waved politely and walked on by. When the third conference came around, I did not attend.

The next year, I learned that this man had been accused of sexual transgressions by dozens of women over several decades.

Following guidance isn't always easy

Trusting intuition can be difficult, even excruciating or heart-breaking. I don't always like, or want to follow, my intuitive guidance. But I've learned that when I do, good things happen.

When my oldest son was sixteen, he got into trouble and was arrested. Upon arriving in Colorado for our annual summer vacation, he said that he wanted to move to Boulder and change his life. So, in addition to helping him with his healing process, I started making arrangements to move.

At the end of the summer, he told me he was thinking about returning to Ohio. The protective Mamma bear inside me screamed "NO!!!!!" And for good reason: The counselor had told me that if he went back, he would have a 95 percent chance of returning to the same lifestyle. I feared for his life.

But, one morning, I woke with a sudden knowing: *He needs to choose for himself.*

I took him to California to sit for a week in council with a dozen Native American elders and encouraged him to seek clarity from his own inner-knowing. On the last night of the retreat, he sat up all night, beating the heartbeat drum through the darkest hours, then entered the sweat lodge just before dawn.

When he emerged from the lodge at sunrise, he'd decided to go back.

My heart broke into a thousand pieces. I wanted a different answer. But my intuition said: *Trust him. His soul knows what it's doing.*

So I prayed and cried, and said yes.

My son never went back to his old life. In the year after his return to Ohio, he earned good grades, won a state championship for high-jumping, and received a scholarship to college.

HOW TO CULTIVATE YOUR INNER KNOWING

Working with intuition means tuning in to very subtle, not-so-obvious "cues and clues," beyond what the rational mind can perceive. You might call it heart-intelligence, intuition, psychic sense, reading energy, or tapping into the Higher Mind.

We have a subtle (psychic) sense that corresponds with every physical sense. Some of the more common and potent senses include clairvoyance (seeing), and clairaudience (hearing), but we also have other psychic senses such as smell, taste, and touch. Intuition is a more general term that refers to the summation of all these psychic senses.

You don't need to be a "psychic" to use intuition; it's a capacity that all humans have, and it can be cultivated through practice. Although sometimes people spontaneously wake up with psychic abilities, typically these gifts take time to develop. Formal training can sharpen these gifts, but it's not necessary.

Basic instructions

First, sit still, slow down, and get very quiet inside. Then, ask a question and listen through your heart for the answer.

Do this by gathering available "data" through your subtle senses. Notice the shifts in your experience, without trying to change anything. Where does your attention go? Do you see images? Hear words? Feel sensations? What's happening in your body—is it opening, closing, melting, shimmering, yearning? What's happening with your emotions—do you feel curious, irritated, sad?

Finally, what meaning do you make of this information? What are these clues trying to tell you? What action seems right to take, based on what you've learned?

Confidence boosters

As you begin to practice working with intuition, try using the following confidence-boosters:

Ask for external signs

The Universe will provide clues if you ask for them. When it was time to put our kitty down after a long struggle with cancer, I was unsure about the right timing, so I asked for a sign. The morning of the scheduled procedure, I stopped in a coffee shop and saw, on a sign (literally on a sign!), the daily special: a "Snickers latte." I had never heard of a Snickers latte ... but my cat's name was Snickers. I left the coffee shop knowing that it was the right day.

Track your results

Intuitive clues are easy to miss if you're not paying attention. When you're learning, it's helpful to keep a log (consider keeping a separate journal, or just noting them in your calendar). This way, you can look back in hindsight and track your accuracy over time. The more you see that your intuition was accurate, the more confidence you'll build.

A colleague once told me that she wanted to find a way to bring me into her business. Although I liked the idea of working with her, I could sense that the timing wasn't right. My intuition said that she would first have to split up with her current partner—and that this would take some time. I made note of this and didn't pursue the opportunity.

A year later, she said, "Guess what!!?? I am breaking up with my business partner. It's going to take a while, but I still want to work with you after we sort it out."

Yep, Intuition smiled. *I knew that.*

BENEDICTION

Trusting inner knowing is more important now than at any other time in history, when the Darkness of climate change, war, and gross inequities threaten to break the fragile balance of human life on Earth.

We cannot continue to operate with blinders on. Blinders can take us down.

And sisters, we are rising. *We are rising.*

Can you feel Sophia, the Goddess of Wisdom calling? She's standing under a sky full of stars, feet firmly planted on the earth, wind blowing through Her hair, holding a torch.

It is the Torch of Truth.

Please, sister, gather your torch and come with me. Let us light many torches, from The One. As wise women connected with our inner knowing, we will find a path through this Darkness and light the way for others.

May it be so. And so, it is.

---

[1] In 2016, "post-truth" was chosen as the Oxford Dictionaries' Word of the Year due to its prevalence in the context of the Brexit referendum and the U.S. presidential election.

[2] According to PolitiFact in July 2017, President Donald Trump was lying 69 percent of the time and only telling the truth 5 percent of the time.

[3] Shadow is a term coined by Carl Jung, referring to unwanted or unconscious aspects of the (individual or collective) psyche.

Allison Conte serves as a bridge between the worlds of work and spirituality. She is an executive coach, organizational consultant, author, and speaker—and a mystic, intuitive, oracle, and spiritual guide. Allison's mission is to help humanity live in harmony with All of Life in ways that honor the Sacred, balance the Masculine and Feminine, and wield power wisely. She works with leaders, coaches, consultants, and entrepreneurs who are committed to being a force for good in the world and who are ready to do the deep inner work required to embody this purpose. As founder of Sophia Leadership, Allison is focused on bringing the Feminine principle into balance with the Masculine principle in organizational leadership and culture. The Sophia Leadership program helps women to lead with more of their innate Feminine essence so they can generate true, sustainable success for themselves and their organizations. Allison currently serves on faculty of the Gestalt Institute of Cleveland. Earlier in her career, she taught on the faculty of the Integral Center and worked as a master executive coach in Case Western Reserve University's Weatherhead School of Management Executive Education Program. Although she considers her spiritual path to be mystical and universal (honoring all wisdom traditions), Allison is deeply devoted to the Sacred Feminine and was ordained as a priestess in the Sophia Lineage in 2013. Since 2000, she has worked with world-class master shamans, spiritual teachers, energy-work masters, and healers. She holds a master's degree in Positive Organization Development from Case Western Weatherhead School of Management, and a bachelor's degree in Journalism from the University of Colorado. She is a certified Spiritual Intelligence Coach. Allison lives in Boulder, Colorado, with her husband, a Christian pastor who captured her heart by welcoming the return of the Divine Feminine in his own tradition. Learn more: **www.sophia-leadership.com** and **www.allisonconte.com**

---

[4] Non-ordinary reality (also called "DreamTime") is a place in consciousness where energy moves, spirits roam, and Magik happens.

[5] The energies of Masculine and Feminine are available to everyone, men and women, regardless of gender; with some exceptions, men typically have easier access to Masculine qualities, and women typically have greater access to the Feminine qualities.

Dancing with my Mother

BY WINDFLOWER COOK

Have you ever danced with your mother? What was it like? Did she lead, or did you? Or did you just dance "together" side by side? My mother's name is Helen and believe me, her name is no accident. Like Helen of Troy, she is the beauty of the family. She is my role model, my hero, my friend and, at times, my biggest critic. She is someone who I would typically think of when I'm dealing with my unresolved emotional issues, at least until recently when I attended an alternative healing class that radically changed my concept of "mother."

The first moment I met Josephine I felt like I already knew her somehow. It's the strangest feeling to be meeting someone for the first time when you feel like you're way past the introductions. I could feel something but I couldn't name it. I couldn't name *what* I was feeling or *why* I was feeling that way. I just felt like something was pulling me toward her. The first spoken interaction with her was, for lack of a better word, *interesting*.

We met at a ThetaHealing® class in Boulder, Colorado, for people who are interested in becoming ThetaHealing practitioners. ThetaHealing is an energy healing modality founded by cancer survivor Vianna Stibal. I'm drawn to it because it empowers people to clear beliefs that no longer serve them so they can take charge of their life in a positive way. It's like quantum physics meets spirituality.

Fifteen people from all over the country took this class, and one left an indelible mark on my heart.

On the third day of class, I was practicing a soul fragments exercise with a classmate, Valerie. In ThetaHealing, soul fragments are like "emotional debris" left over from relationships. Think of it like an energetic exchange, either negative or positive, often resulting in an energetic pull on the psyche. The exercise is to pull back through a meditative state, or the person's soul fragments from this past partnership, and bring back all of the exchanges passed between the two people. It's simpler than it sounds.

Valerie and I explored this exchange for about twenty minutes before Josephine told us, rather matter of factly, "The exercise is over." There was no question in her tone; she exudes self-confidence. Self-confidence is something I've never had. I've wanted it, craved it, and tried to earn it anyway I could. But with Josephine, I found myself comparing us and I'd come up short. *Why am I comparing myself to her?* I asked myself. *Like she knows best? Like she's like my mother?* I raise my hand to ask a question. "We really need to move on," Josephine says with authority. "We've got a lot to cover." *Why doesn't she want to answer my question?* I wonder. I feel frustrated that she doesn't want to take a few minutes to address what I am wondering about.

And then the big question: *Why do I feel like I'm not worthy?*

I'm suddenly aware of how I'm taking all of this personally. Something is triggering these emotions. It feels like mother stuff. My inner dialogue continues with a whole judge and jury going on in my head. My mother *is* like Josephine. They are both confident, strong, and self-assured. My mother is a lawyer, and you know what that means. She's right 99 percent of the time. If you have something to say, it better be good. There is only so much time and time is valuable. The law is on her side. Add that to Helen of Troy beauty! It's hard to measure up to that.

Partway through the day I run across Valerie in the restroom. She looks concerned. "Windy," she says, "Josephine just told me that you and I carried some incomplete energetic connection from the last exercise into the classroom."

"What?" I say, sounding nervous.

"Yes," she says. "We have to finish something."

I am triggered again, I realize as thoughts circle in my head. *I feel like I didn't accomplish what we needed to get done, I've failed ... oh no ... like how it feels when your mother points her finger at you and says you didn't do something right.*

When I see Josephine my shoulders tighten. "Josephine, what did you tell Valerie?" I ask.

"You and Valerie have to complete your exercise," Josephine explains.

"We did," I say with a serious tone.

"I think you both need to return to the exercise and possibly finish whatever you started," she replies. She sounds genuinely concerned.

I realize that she's being helpful, or trying to be helpful, and my feelings about her don't have anything to do with Josephine. My feelings are about my relationship with my mother … the relationship that I now have with my two daughters.

Do soul fragments pertain to daughters and mothers, too?

I wonder if sometimes as children we have experiences with our mothers that become energetic debris that triggers you and "pulls you when they are unresolved."

Why *wouldn't* there be an energetic pull? The relationship with our mother is the *first* relationship we have with someone other than ourselves. That's powerful. In utero, we are encapsulated as one being, but at birth we are two separate people. Beginning together, growing together and then ultimately separating into two independent people. How do we separate? What does it look like? And when we do, how does it affect us?

At lunch with my classmates at a nearby cafe, I feel lightheaded, not at all grounded. Josephine comments that possibly all of the crystals I'm wearing could be the reason. I look down and I've got a large quartz crystal necklace, a quartz pyramid bracelet and crystal earrings on. Instantly, I feel foolish, like I'm doing something I shouldn't be doing … again. *I'm wearing crystals and not wearing them right.* I'm feeling that mother trigger.

"You should take them off and put them in the sunlight by the rock garden here," Josephine says. And I do as she's suggested. But I can't help but observe how I'm triggered again. I don't get triggered this often by someone. *What is going on here?* I ask myself.

My stomach growls and my eyes scan the menu as I think about what I want to eat. I look over to see Josephine and I'm curious as to what she is ordering. *Why do I want to know what she's going to eat? Don't I know what I want to eat?* Josephine is so confident, self-assured and she obviously knows more than I do. Oh there it is again. I notice this energetic pull toward Josephine.

A classmate who's been quietly observing my interactions with Josephine, whispers, "You and Josephine have shared quite a few lifetimes together."

I gasp, "What! Oh my God."

No one has ever told me something like that. What does that mean? Why does that feel so significant? Do people continue to share lifetimes together because they have something to learn from each other?

Is it a dance? Mother and daughter? Do mothers and daughters dance together throughout time? Do two people interact over and over again, to learn from each other, teach each other, understand each other, to evolve?

"Josephine, did you hear that?"

Josephine nods yes, and then I say something that surprises her. I ask her what her middle name is. I often think that a person's middle name reflects a person's past life. It's like a clue.

"My middle name is Helen," she says.

I get those goosebumps all over as I respond, "That is my Mother's name."

She looks stunned for a moment, then says, "Okay, now that explains why I get triggered by you."

"What do you mean?"

"I don't know how to explain it, but it's like I want to comfort you like a mother would," Josephine says. "I also notice that you act less confident when you are around me like you devalue yourself in my presence and that really annoys me."

"Really?" I say. "I do that around you?"

Just like with my mother in this lifetime, I think to myself.

"Yes," Josephine says, looking thoughtful. "You do that, and I don't know why. You are obviously a very powerful woman but you seem to become less confident around me."

And then it comes to me.

"You were my mother in a past life, maybe several past lives ... and maybe I was your mother," I say with a charged tone of voice.

"Yes," she says.

My understanding of mother at that very moment changed. It was no longer the linear idea "I am the daughter of Helen and she is my mother" but was now multi-faceted and dynamic: She is my mother in this lifetime because I have an important lesson to understand, a lesson that I've possibly spent many lifetimes examining.

Do we choose our mother, spiritually speaking, each lifetime to replay a dynamic that we need to look at, ponder and reject, or honor? I don't know. What I am beginning to understand is this one powerful relationship shapes our identity, our self-concept, and our thoughts. And my concept of this sacred relationship of mother and daughter has changed.

What was to happen next with my own daughter highlighted my new concept of "mother" and highlighted how I had changed … how my own *awareness* of this sacred relationship had evolved. This is central to who I am, being a mother to three children: a ten-year-old girl and five-year-old fraternal twins. One morning, my oldest daughter, Aubrielle, complained of a terrible stomach. She told me that she couldn't go to school because she felt nauseous and probably had a stomach flu.

Having just completed my ThetaHealing practitioner training, I asked her to sit down on the couch and get comfortable. I asked her if I could understand her problem from a higher perspective. She agreed with a half-smile and laid back down on the couch. After I went into the Theta State, which is a very relaxed, meditative state and asked the question, I received an answer. I told her the reason she wasn't feeling well: because she's worried.

"What, you can read minds?" she asked.

"No, I didn't read your mind," I assured her. "I put the question out to the universe, and I received an answer."

She squinted at me as I continued explaining.

"I did a reading. I asked The Creator of All that Is to tell me why you have a stomach ache."

"Who is Creator?"

"Creator is any title you want to give the Creative Force of the universe or pure energy of All That Is. In other words, Creator is what we know of the Divine Energy. You can call this anything you want, the Great Spirit, God, Buddha, Jesus, Shiva, Goddess, Yahweh, Allah …"

She nodded.

"You are worried about your school project," I said. "You are worried you will disappoint your school partner—and me."

I've certainly felt that, not wanting to disappoint my mother! And what Josephine had triggered in me was basically the same thing that was making Aubrielle feel worried.

I felt sad, mad, uneasy and immediately needed to reassure myself. I needed to "feel okay" and not just "okay" but amazing. I needed to feel I was amazing because "okay" was never good enough for my mother, Helen of Troy, the daughter of Zeus. My mind began to rewind searching for something in my past to make myself feel better. I looked back at how I always got straight A's and how I earned not just one but two master's degrees. I reminded myself of my past professions as a former family therapist, elementary school teacher, and social worker so I could take pride in myself as a great mother.

At that moment, I felt insecure. I needed to remind myself of how patient, kind, and devoted I was as a mother. I became conscious of what I needed to face. I needed to face that I have always felt inferior to my powerful, beautiful mother. The bar was set so high when I was a child and I never could measure up. That feeling of never measuring up hit me hard and it hurt. Like when you get the wind knocked out of you. The pull to Josephine was the same pull I've felt with my mother, as if in striving to be more like her I could be more powerful myself.

And my daughter was reflecting this back at me, like a mirror.

I asked her if I could understand her feelings of worry with her permission so she could feel better. She agreed, and I closed my eyes, took a deep breath, relaxed, went into the Theta State and asked *where* in Aubrielle's being is the thought if she doesn't accomplish something, she will disappoint someone. I could see the thought pattern emanating from two places in her body, the sides of her head and her shoulders. According to the ThetaHealing technique, this thought pattern was occurring in our family ancestry and in her past lives. For me, this confirmed the recent interaction of being triggered as far as my mother issues that I had with Josephine.

This mother-daughter pattern of receiving conditional love and attention based on accomplishments was occurring in Aubrielle's ancestors (which included me, my mother Helen, my grandmother Libby, etc.) throughout time.

I flashed on a conversation I once had with my mother. "In my family," my mother told me, "you had to 'do,' you had to rise to your potential, and strive for greatness to be recognized and given attention." She had ten siblings, she reminded me, and, "you had to stand out to be noticed. I remember one night I didn't go to the dinner table. I wanted to see if anyone noticed I wasn't there."

"Did anyone notice?" I asked her.

"Yes, my mother finally called my name. I was glad she called my name."

Remembering this conversation, I looked at Aubrielle and I wanted her to feel loved by *just being*. Just being. Something I didn't feel as a child with my own mother.

At that moment, I understood the energetic pull I experienced with Josephine and with my own mother. *If I don't accomplish something I will disappoint,* I'd be trained to think. But if we're all spiritually connected and we clear a thought pattern in one person, it not only helps the individual but the group collective consciousness as well.

I reflected again on the concept of soul fragments and how it could possibly offer us a clue into the energetic pull that we have as mothers and as daughters. My energetic pull to Josephine and to my mother is to receive praise or acknowledgment that I've accomplished something so I can be "noticed" and receive love. For the first time, I could see it clearly. Crystal clear.

Ultimately, we have to separate from our mother, differentiate from her, and think for ourselves, but at the same time we need to look up to her, emulate her, and respond to the world as if she's within us. Mother. She's what we aspire to be like, or in some instances, just parts of her that we aspire to be like. When we become a mother ourselves, we have the opportunity to embrace the best version of our mother and leave behind the rest. It's like a dance. A dance in which we are aware of each other, connecting to the rhythm of life, embracing each other but allowing each other to freely move in our own beautiful, unique way.

On the third day of the ThetaHealing workshop, we practiced clearing rejection, regret, and resentment. Josephine said she wanted to work on clearing resentment. Josephine said that she feels resentment toward her mother and father for their lack of support when she first became a mother to a baby girl years ago. We began the exercise by taking a deep breath and going into a calm, relaxed state. This exercise was to finally resolve Josephine's feelings of resentment toward her parents around not being emotionally supported when she became a new mother. I asked a question, "How can Josephine feel supported now, in this moment?"

An answer was given to my question. In place of resentment was a dance. A dance came to me, and I willingly acted it out. I became Josephine's mother, and I opened up my arms and embraced her from her solar plexus. I stood in front of her, and another student embodied Josephine's father by embracing her from behind like strong pillars at her back. We hugged Josephine from both sides, and together, we began to sway back and forth. We began to dance. We danced as mother and daughter, and daughter and mother. *The dance was the embodiment of unconditional love and support.* Josephine began to cry and it was a good cry. A cleansing cry of forgiveness.

In that moment, I realized that my own mother also felt alone when she became a new mother to me. My concept of mother has changed. It has evolved. I don't perceive my mother, Helen, as responsible for my issues anymore. The truth is I chose her. I chose her so that I could see in myself what I need to work on. What I needed to work on is that it's enough to *just be*. I am beautiful, strong, amazing, intelligent, and powerful by just being. It's my divine right. It's not what I do, how I look, or what I accomplish. "Just being," as I like to call it, is this dance of changing roles, sometimes leading and sometimes following.

My "Helen of Troy" is *me*. She is my role model, my friend, and my mirror. I see in her what I admire, what I want to honor in myself, and what I want to change. Just like a dance. Being a mother to my children enables me to understand this evolution in a deeper, more profound way. As a mother, I love embodying self-confidence, self-assurance, and strength to my daughter, much of what my mother exuded to me. Now I know the self-confidence comes from *within*. From the inside out!

In this *new* dance as a mother to Aubrielle, I am leading, at least right now. I am leading by loving her for *just being,* without the focus on *how* we dance, how beautiful we look, or what we *accomplish* in our dancing. Being free of the energetic pull to receive love for accomplishments such as when "one steps out of line." This new dance is about joy, spontaneity, genuine support, and unconditional love.

And, with my mother, Helen, it's time for a new dance. This time we dance together side by side, moving in our own way, having fun, and it feels good. I feel *free*.

Windflower Cook is a mom of three children, former family therapist, Special Olympics volunteer, physio-neuro trainer, social worker, Reiki II practitioner, and elementary school teacher. She is also a humanitarian, animal rights activist, and feminist. She is the author of Following Windy, an interactive online blog at "Moms Like Me" and author of Sisterhood of the Modern Goddess *published by Flower of Life Press. She can also be found in a nearby yoga studio, hiking, playing with her children, picking wildflowers,*  *walking her dog, or riding her pink cruiser in open space. Windflower has a master's degree of Social Work from the University of Denver and a master's degree in Educational Psychology from the University of Colorado, Denver. She recently became certified as a Basic DNA and Advanced ThetaHealing® Practitioner and as a Basic ThetaHealing Instructor. Windy is currently developing a non-profit with her vision to help raise the consciousness on the planet. She lives in Louisville, Colorado with her husband of fifteen years, three children and a big golden retriever. Contact Windflower at **windy_beth@yahoo.com**.*

Remembering the Divine Feminine: A Mystic Momma's Journey

BY DANA DAMARA

I've been fascinated with the Divine Feminine for years. I heard the phrase when I was in my thirties, in an unhappy marriage, trying to pretend everything was perfect behind the white picket fence, the gorgeous husband, and two beautiful daughters. The word just rolled off my tongue one day when I was practicing yoga in my family room. I was feeling very off balance with two children under the age of four. While balancing in Ardha Chandrasana, I found myself saying, "The Divine Feminine supports and sustains me." I remember looking around and thinking, *Wow, where did that come from?*

That sweet voice never went away—it only got stronger over the years. Since then I've unraveled my life to match the call in my heart toward this energy we call the Divine Feminine.

I think it's important to first define Divine Feminine:

One who directly relates to her Source energy. The energy of Shakti that defines all movement on this planet. That lives and breathes as all living things. The energy that not only creates but destroys, and receives. The Divine Feminine is not just a female dressed in white, with flowers and jewels dripping from her limbs and flying from her hair—although that is indeed a beautiful way to embody what may look like the Divine Feminine. It means remembering our interconnection and oneness; it's remembering that everyone and everything we experience is a reflection of the inner balance of the masculine and feminine. The Moon IS the Divine Feminine and we are most definitely connected to the Moon. To embody the Divine Feminine means remembering who you are, and that means all sides of self, the masculine and the feminine—in all your fullness. It means embracing it all. That Divine balance of Shiva and Shakti. When YOU embrace all sides of yourself, others can too.

I have finally owned my own Divine Feminine and the strength, struggles, integrity, gratitude, and grace that path entails. It hasn't been easy or without multiple course corrections. I am a single mother raising two teenage daughters in Marin County, California—a community that offers amazing opportunities but also experiences extreme affluenza. Day after day, I witness my own reflection in my girls and use the practice of yoga to harness any projections I may be tossing around and to them. It's a daily effort, that's for sure. Together, we navigate social media, drugs, alcohol, the public school system, their own worth, their parents' divorce, and of course what it means to be a teenager in today's world. It's not easy for them. And, even with this practice of yoga and meditation, my projections still come out somehow:

Why doesn't their father live here? Why isn't he here for them? Why am I sacrificing my happiness for theirs? Am I good enough to be on the cover of Yoga Journal? *And why do I want that anyway? Why am I still alone? What do I really have to offer?*

I review and reflect on my life and offerings disguised as lessons and outdated patterns that continue to show up. I pause throughout my day, I cry on my yoga mat, I cuddle with my children, I speak my truth, and I do my best to find balance. And … my compass still finds ways to get out of alignment. Thanks to the breath, the internal knowledge and expression of the Divine, I come back quickly.

The reality is that we are dense beings of light. This Earth suit that we walk around in both protects us and gets us where we need to go every day. But we are more than this Earth suit. So when we unravel anything, we must unravel all levels of our being. My yoga practice brought me to gazing at the Moon, the Planets and the Stars. It brought me to Shakti and Shiva and what that really means. It reminded me that even if we can't see it, we can still ground into the collective breath. Once I put myself in alignment with the Moon and Her rhythms, my life took on a hum that was similar to the sound of *Om*. It rang from the center of my being and there was flow.

The Moon cycles are real; nature is real, and it's chaotic and messy and unpredictable. Our job is to stand tall in that "mess" and BE who we are meant to be. To continually align ourselves with the essence of the Mother, of the Divine … beyond our stories, beyond our pain, beyond the players that reflect to us who we are being in that moment. We are meant to remember—to *re*-member who we are, and that is Divine.

With deep compassion for my childhood, a foundation of balance, safety, security, pleasure, joy, empowerment, unconditional love, truth, intuition, and connection to Divine Source was not something modeled in my home. No one ever told me I could cycle with the Moon! No one ever told me to use my intuition … I just did it.

Thankfully I was born with it. It was just something I knew existed.

Gratefully, I found yoga, meditation, and my breath. And even now, I still can get snagged in the illusion of separateness and forget how to wield my power. To this day, I can get caught up in the idea of not-enoughness and doubt my own worthiness to fully dance with the Divine! Because the world shows us differently. The world shows us what we *think we are missing*. It tells us that we are damaged, not enough, and need something or someone to complete us and make us whole.

If you were raised with that belief system, it will be your work to see otherwise. And if you have children, *especially daughters*, it will be your work to support them in rewriting those patterns and eradicating those thoughts, so they no longer live inside them either.

I was raised to be quiet unless I was spoken to. That my ideas and thoughts didn't matter. That the only way I could get attention was if I did something radically out of the box. That I was unworthy of unconditional love and appreciation. That the angrier I got, the more power I had. That having an abortion was the most shameful thing any woman could ever do to herself. That you needed a man to make life work in a family setting, no matter the cost. That if you didn't like a situation, the best thing to do was to leave and get as far away as you could. That the more numbed out I was, the less it mattered. I was taught to point the finger out and to keep my mouth shut because I was a disgrace to the family. The things I had done, no one ever did before, and if anyone in the family found out, it would be horrific.

I held onto that neglect, abandonment, shame, and unworthiness for a long time. I was, at one point, a little girl who was ignored and abused by her father. A young teenager who was wronged by many men. A young woman who ran away from anything that looked remotely like a potential commitment because it would, for sure, at some point in time, unravel and she would be left alone. Better to leave than be the one being left … right?

This was the story anyway.

The anger I held toward my father was so deep I watched it play out in relationship after relationship. It was with me for so long and lodged inside me so deeply that there was no way that anyone NOT like my father could ever show up.

Here's the consequence of harboring anger: If you are angry with the masculine and you march against them, if you speak in angry tones against them, then you are angry with yourself and speaking to yourself. If you cut yourself off from the feminine to "make things happen," you are out of balance.

When you hold onto that anger toward anyone, it is a ripple that is detrimental to all.

When you hide, shield, or pretend to be something less, you cannot obtain balance. Instead, you create a loathing or shameful existence for yourself. Not willing to accept all sides breeds shame for who you are and attracts less than your birthright has to offer.

But the Divine Goddess knows that all is well. That there are multiple lifetimes. That our life is a spiral and if it is not time, it is not time. She doesn't get angry, she just sits. And breathes. That is the Goddess—the Feminine, the Moon, Shakti. And that is the only way for me now.

A balance of Shiva and Shakti in your way of breathing, speaking, and being is necessary. And while this sounds easy enough, the truth is that we are all out of balance and disconnected from our inner Shiva/Shakti. We all continue to play in the realm of "finding" balance and we do it through our health, our lifestyle, our choices, our relationships, and our healing.

It's a remembering that we are supported by Father Sky and Mother Earth equally. And that all elements, directions, and seasons of our life are integral in honoring our path.

I believe this CAN be called The Path of a Priestess, however, my concern with the word *Priestess* is that some definitions renounce relationship with the masculine. When we renounce relationship with the masculine willingly, we renounce that relationship within ourselves, which only perpetuates the imbalance.

The Divine Feminine, however, marches alongside all people—and She does so with a heart that's open wide and a vessel for all. She does so not to march against anything or to prove anything but to bring people together so that they may see the power of Oneness.

But no one ever told me ... so I spent a large part of my life believing something different. Until now.

The truth was that this young girl was magic and intuitive and something special, but no one ever told her. This teenager was actually feared by young boys and girls because the power she held was palpable, nothing like anyone in her group had seen before. This young woman was loved so deeply by her husband, but she was so guarded that she never knew, because she never let anyone in close enough to see her heart. This angel possessed a light that no one knew how to work with so they tried to ignore it, hide it, and put it out—at all costs.

And as you know, once a story has been told, the mind will do everything it can to continue to perpetuate that story so it holds validation. It will continue to send player after player until that sweet soul can't do anything but admit defeat. It's much easier than fighting. If nothing besides validation of shame, fear, guilt, grief, and lies shows up, that is all the soul will believe.

In the quest for growth, the fight must come from a place of yearning for evolution, not domination, fear, or control. But sometimes there's just not time for evolution ... or joy ... or happiness. There's only surviving, right?

Wrong.

When I changed my verbiage from "I *deserve* to be loved unconditionally, be adored and live in joy and contentment" to "It is my *birthright* to be loved unconditionally, be adored and live in joy and contentment," it became much easier to allow into my belief system.

There is something we all must remember:

There is only one person in the room. We are mere reflections of each other. So when I believe that "someone else" isn't paying enough attention to me, isn't that a statement of how much attention I'm simply not giving myself?

The process that began unraveling my belief of not-enoughness and unworthiness was recognizing what was attracting all of this in the first place, and then *owning it.*

Yes, owning it.

Pain, anger, resentment, attachment to a story ... who would I be without all of these things? How would I function if I was Divine? Would people be attracted to me if I was normal? What would I talk about if it wasn't my pain? I had attracted so much based on that old story. What was underneath it? I had been carrying it around for so long ... what would happen if I dropped it and just became someone who actually did love and live life fully?

These stories shaped me for years. I lived with these lies all the way into my early forties. And let's be honest, I *chose* to hold onto those stories; no one made me. Why? Because I couldn't answer these questions:

Who would I be without those stories? Who would I be without my pain? Who would I be without my past abuse and suffering? What story would I really have to tell?

So the stories took root and I carried them around like a badge of honor. In actuality, all they did was guard me from finding myself—which meant, in the bigger picture, shielding myself from finding relationships that truly served my soul.

The relationships I experienced were instead a reflection of my own unworthiness and deeply seeded belief that I was not enough. And if I put myself out there—the one I *wanted* everyone to see—then maybe I would be worthy of unconditional love and adoration. That was the root of the weed I kept trying to pull and eradicate from my garden. But it was embedded so deeply that it kept coming up.

My soul wanted to sing and I knew I had more to offer. After fifteen years I was dying inside by playing so small.

So I made a hard right turn.

It's an act of bravery to let go of a story and stand in the light of the Divine. It's something that requires daily effort, work and full attention to your thoughts, words and actions.

Thankfully, after a divorce, bankruptcy, closing my business, leaving my kids with their dad while I set up a new life in California, and starting my career over in San Francisco at age forty-four, I was ready to put myself out there again—only in a bigger and brighter way.

Now, I can answer these questions:

Who would I be without those old stories? Who would I be without my pain? Who would I be without my past abuse and suffering? What story would I really have to tell?"

Without these stories, I AM:
- A strong, capable, flexible being full of radiance and light.
- Invincible.
- Forever young.
- Adaptable, awake and alive.
- Living in the present moment and connected to all that is happening in the Now.
- Clear in thoughts that are Divinely guided instead of experience clouded.
- Pristine, virgin-like, open and vulnerable.
- Forever forgiving and infinitely trusting of my own Self.

Our path is not a straight line … it is a spiral of energy that brings lessons to us over and over again so we can regain balance and heal. And hopefully, as we spiral through our lives, like the planets spiral through the universe, we notice the lessons that continually show up for us. Hopefully, along our journey we have gained more tools to forgive, heal, and move forward as a stronger version of the Divine Feminine in balance.

Remind yourself often:
- Allowing others to take your power is not the way of the Divine Feminine.
- Blaming others is not the way of the Divine Feminine.
- Projecting your anger and frustration onto others is not the way of the Divine Feminine.
- Staying in a relationship that does not serve your highest good is not the way of the Divine Feminine.

Of course, She *can* be seen dressed in flowy white gowns, jewels on her forehead, dancing around a fire with Her besties in the middle of the forest, spewing magical words and living in bliss. But the best way to locate Her is in the struggles or the lessons.

- She is the executive speaking her truth in a conference room full of men.
- She is the mother guiding and challenging her children.
- She is the man who supports his partner and lives and breathes in equal reciprocity.
- She is the student making her way through her first day of college.
- She is the political activist who marches with compassion and empowerment.
- She is the one who stands up for what's real with words that are laced in truth and consideration.

We must remember that *Divine Feminine* is a phrase that is accessible to everyone, right now. It is not some airy-fairy concept that only "women circles" and "priestesses" can access. When we think that way, we live in separation, again. No, the Divine Feminine is pulsing in all of us ... right now. So my invitation to you is to notice where YOU witness the Divine Feminine in your day to day life.

And that is where the journey starts and ends ... with full appreciation and gratitude for it all. With clean and clear energy powered by the breath and deep awareness to the Divine Play of life, knowing the power our hands have in it but remembering not to control any of it.

Your healing modalities are powerful. What relationships you choose make a huge difference in your healing. Be awake to all relationships ... every single one. They are a reflection of *you* ... every single time. You get to choose which relationships are for you and which ones are not. Each one holds a lesson that you get to recognize when it's complete.

In relationship, you *dance with your karmic path and learn to forgive over and over again until you regain balance.* And the good news is that it's a life-long process, so if you are still here, you are still finding balance. Embracing and owning the lessons is the quickest way to healing.

It is your birthright to allow and receive prosperity, love and bliss. And it is your job to unravel the binds that keep you stuck in thinking that you are any less than your Divine light of Being—which means taking responsibility for them and not ignoring them or projecting them onto others.

This is done with compassion, grace, unconditional love, and the necessity of a tribe—*a group of powerful individuals who hold you in the container of truth, freedom and love while you sift around through the scattered pieces of yourself and find the pearl that holds it all together.*

Unworthiness and not-enoughness serve no one and certainly don't serve your soul's calling. When you hold feelings of unworthiness, you stay small or you burn out, depending on how you play that out in your life.

We are dense beings, so when we unravel the lessons we must do so on several levels: the physical, mental, subtle, emotional, and energetic. We must clear, eradicate, cleanse, and dissolve as much static in our vessel as possible so we can hear the call from the Divine and hear it daily. And that doesn't mean we are perfect. We practice and we play.

In this process of unraveling old beliefs of unworthiness, shame, fear, guilt, grief, and attachment, I have found that there is more time to breathe into the Divine. I have found that my heart expands and my clairvoyance becomes attuned. When we know our worth, we can see above the drama and choose not to engage. And when we know our worth we can make decisions based on what's happening in our life without looking outside of ourselves.

We see the relationships in our lives as lessons and not even anyone outside of ourselves. We can then become completely sovereign from their actions and understand it's their karma working itself out. We stop spending our time trying to change people or anything outside ourselves, because all we ever need to be concerned with is the message we're sending out with our thoughts, words, and deeds.

So if you feel scattered, pull your prana in. Evaluate where your energy is leaking … where are you spending your time? Where are you expending your energy? With whom? How? Is it depleting you? If so, it may be time to let something go so you can regain connection to Source—*your* Source. By pulling in your prana, you regain balance, attune your channel, and have the chance to recalibrate.

Break through illusion ... at all costs. Illusions are created by the ego to keep you stagnate or stuck in some pattern. The goal is to recognize the pattern and see where *you* have played a role in this. Where have you created a story that you're replaying in order to gain a deeper knowing of yourself? The best way to shatter illusion is to sit, breathe, and ask. And then, listen. Intently. Listen with your entire body, not with your ears. Pay attention to every single sign and then drop what isn't real. You know what it is, you just have to trust that when you drop it, truth will prevail.

And please, for the love of Goddess, offer up unconditional love. And not just with the easy targets but with the challenging ones too. Maybe with yourself first—that can sometimes be the most challenging soul to love.

Remember that you are whole. You are Divine. You are a balance of masculine and feminine and you must love it all, even if it takes several breaths and hundreds of yoga practices to get there.

Balance. That is my definition of the Divine Feminine.

Dana Damara is one of the Bay Area's premier yoga instructors and a leading advocate for women and young girl empowerment. She is a mystic, a mother, a teacher of teachers, and an author. She traverses between the mystical realms and real-life drama of a mother of two teenage girls. She is an activist for women of all ages: committed to feminine embodiment, self-love, sisterhood, sacred ceremony and ritual, and creating a safe space for evolution. When she's not leading one of her fiery Moon Mystic Classes, she  *may be facilitating a retreat, hosting a women's Moon Circle, empowering her clients, creating an inseparable tribe with her Embody Truth Teacher Training program, or simply hanging out with her daughters during down time from school. She believes that the body has many depths. What happens on the outside is simply a reflection of what is going on inside. It's just a matter of how awake we are to that wisdom. Kama, Artha, and Dharma must be in alignment in order to be liberated from the lower levels of negativity that keeps us stuck. If we want liberation, we must do the work, and it is all based on self-inquiry, exploration, and discovery.* "On the mat, my passion is proper alignment, powerful breath and effortless flow," *Damara says.* "Time on your mat is sacred space where you find more depth, authenticity, and integrity in your life." *She believes that how you show up on your mat can be directly related to how you show up off your mat.* "When we begin to integrate this truth and see ourselves with compassionate awareness," *she says,* "we are liberated from any illusion that holds us back from moving out into the world." *Learn more:* **DanaDamara.com**

I Choose Love

BY ELAYNE KALILA DOUGHTY

It's a cold winter's night. There's a circle of us gathering to take a powerful medicine journey together.

I sit quietly to feel into what the intention of my journey will be and then hear a voice deep inside—very clearly—with some force, ask:

Do you choose to walk as love?

"This is too simple, too obvious," I think.

The same voice returns and I settle into the invitation.

"Okay, fine. I choose Love."

······⟡······

Surrendering to the music, I breathe deeply and feel the journey rising.

A kaleidoscope of images begin to open in front of me like a moving book; pages turn at light speed.

Scene after scene shows my life—like a movie—interacting with all the people I know and love. It seems like a life review.

I look closer and see, much to my discomfort, all the ways I have not been loving to myself, to others, to the world. I mean: ALL the ways.

There are volumes of these "movie books"—a seemingly never-ending cascade of images, feelings, felt senses—of fleeting moments where I judged my lover for losing the way and not being able to navigate or not being able to multi-task like me. Or where I judge him for not being "like me" or doing it the way that I would—which is obviously the better way to do whatever it might be—you get the picture …

The images show where I separate myself from other women and use judgment as a way to shield my awkward feelings of not belonging. Or where I choose to hide out and stay in my comfort zone rather than reach toward another who may need love in this moment …

I see when I feel hurt by something a sister friend says … and instead of turning toward her in intimacy, I shut down and protect my heart, all while appearing to stay connected.

I'm shown the time I turned away from the homeless man standing at the traffic intersection instead of offering him my presence when he asked for money.

When I am "too busy" to truly listen to what you might be sharing with me from your deepest heart.

And I see the moment when my lover is unavailable to me, so I become angry and withhold my love because I didn't get what I wanted.

The images continue tumbling through me.

I see when I have been self-serving and selfish while wanting to appear loving and giving: When I claimed I was loving, yet underneath, was not … like when I said and did things in the temple that were veiled with love but hid feelings of frustration, impatience, and judgment.

My heart rate is going up, but the pages keep turning.

I feel horrified.

It's like I'm being shown the energetic picture of how I move in the world at extremely subtle levels, unmasking where I stop or shut down the flow of love.

And there are a lot of ways … a lot.

A lot.

......✂......

I am exhausted.

I'm being called to examine every single relationship in my life and see—without masks and veils—what is real.

I am learning what love ISN'T.

I see how I subtly veil my superiority … and how much of my time I am still in a comparison mind set.

I see how often I spend my life in fear, constriction … not-enoughness and scarcity.

I see how easily I have been seduced into being successful.

Oh, the trappings of living as a "modern priestess" and all the glamors that can—and do—pull me out of alignment with love!

I am literally on my knees feeling tattered, torn, and humbled beyond belief from being shown all that was hidden in my subconscious. Hidden from my view.

This deeply painful, nauseating, and relentless replay is ego annihilating.

Even things I thought were truly loving are held up for review and dis-integrate into a flimsy veil of nothingness.

I need to lay down.

I feel crumbled knowing how I have fallen short of who I thought I was and aspire to be.

All I can do is lie in the fetal position defeated. Completely done.

There is this feeling of loneliness that overcomes me and I am bereft.

Now, the real agony sets in as I see new pictures of how I repeatedly denied loving myself.

My body shakes with tears.

I vomit.

Cry.

There are so many ways I have abandoned and mistreated myself.

I see how hard I push myself for the "mission" of supporting others …

how often I turn away from my tiredness, needs, and limits, still pushing along in a mean and judgmental way.

I have avoided feeling my tenderness through the shields of a very old pattern that judges weakness. The patriarchy is embedded in my cells: the punishment, the harshness, the shaming of my own feminine nature.

I see how I turned away from Mother—from Her within me—even though I have chosen devotion to Her.

As I watch these images, my failings become clear to me and … then I judge myself more. It is venomous and I feel the poison of being stuck in this eternal cycle of violence within myself.

How is it that this could be so hidden?

It's as though I'm dismembered.

I land at the bottom of my inner cave with nowhere to go.

⸱⸱⸱⸱⸱⸱⧓⸱⸱⸱⸱⸱⸱

Somehow, in this darkness, I become lucid of Inanna and Her journey into the underworld while being hung on a meat hook for three days.

I am hanging on the hook. Rotting.

And, for a moment, I feel some kind of sweet relief.

I'm surrendered, unmasked, no longer hidden from myself.

I am intimate with my inner-most chamber.

Here, there is a sweet innocence that begins streaming through me as I feel the tenderness of dying to myself.

⸱⸱⸱⸱⸱⸱⧓⸱⸱⸱⸱⸱⸱

I become aware of a hand on the back of my neck, holding my head like a baby, embracing me in a powerful presence.

I know Her.

It is the Magdalene.

I feel Her breathing love into my heart, rewiring my body with a new circuitry within my entire energetic and nervous systems.

The warmth of golden light rushes through my body. And with a release, it's as if everything I saw and experienced is being cleansed, purified in this enormous presence of love.

······◦❦◦······

This love is one I have never conceived of before.

It rushes like a forceful river through my being.

A love that is strong, sure, powerful. Fierce, tender, and passionate.

It's the imprint of liberation: uncompromising, ever-present, unwavering.

Love—a fire that burns brightly, pure and unconditional. Insistent and urgent. Patient and kind.

Love that is a force.

Love that is not compromised.

Love that embracingly holds the light and the shadow.

Love that speaks truth with compassion.

Love that stands with the sword of integrity and has the courage—the heart—to stay true.

Love that loves: no matter what.

······◦❦◦······

I lay in Her arms breathing Her breath.

I feel myself become one with Her, our bodies merging together into union.

And I know that the version of love I have been so cavalier about before the ceremony is indeed the only thing I am here to master and come to know.

Whatever I had "thought" was love prior to this moment does not even touch what Divine Love truly is.

······◦❦◦······

So, I vow to turn towards.

There is nowhere else to go.

......ॐ......

I hear the Magdalene say:

For your presence is love.

Ain Soph Aur. Ain Soph Aur. Ain Soph Aur.
Limitless Light. Limitless Light. Limitless Light.

The quintessence of choosing Love is found in the choice to be present with yourself first. And in so doing, you cultivate your inner PRESENCE.

This is a radical and beautiful path of intimacy and the Heart of the Magdalene.

LIGHT-PRESENCE-LOVE.

You are THAT.

You are LOVE.

Ain Soph Aur.

You have been a well-kept secret even from yourself.

Your most intimate truth is that you have jewels shining within you that are rare and precious in their configuration. Each one of us has our own imprint.

And in this moment, you are being called forward to reveal the secret, to unveil the secret that you have long held within our dark wombs, within the caves where you were safe to hide.

You are now being called to step out in the resplendence of all that you are, holding NOTHING BACK, so you can stream limitless light of Love from your vessel.

HOLD NO-THING back.

Ain Soph Aur.

Break past the limitations of the old story that you have to be this or that, or that you either have to be sinner or saint, or victim or perpetrator.

You are in the land of something extraordinary.

Through the alchemy of love in your heart, you can bring all that is not love into love.

Simple.

All that has been exiled in the darkness, is to be embraced in the elixir of LOVE.

Breathe in this light.

You are here to walk a unifying consciousness at this time that balances the old story that we have been told that there are only two options to be the exalted: The light OR the shadow.

You are here to walk in the simplicity that there is a new story being told not from our words or our actions, but from our presence ... through your resonance and presence, through your willingness to walk as love.

To take the vow to BE love.

THIS IS NOT A TEACHING, BUT AN EXPERIENCE.

We are all called to drop the complexity of mind that becomes confused so easily when we are challenged to step in our divine humanity instead of allowing our hearts to open to what we know.

We are here now to hold this kind of resonance.

Resonance is the key that unlocks our hidden treasures to shine forth in simple quintessential glory, with no pomp and circumstance, but with a drum roll that heralds in an age of Kings and Queens within all of our hearts.

It is that simple.

Resonance feels.
Resonance amplifies in the heart.
Resonance is found in simple, open-hearted presence.

Are you willing to BE presence?

Ain Soph Aur.

Are you willing to let the crystalline being of your body light up with so much brilliance that you shine light effortlessly, because it is who are you as a quintessence?

Beloved.
Turn towards everything.
Yes, even that which you despise and revile against.
Open your heart.
Empty your mind.

Drop into stillness for a moment, the place where all things come into unity within you.
Turn towards your own heart.
Feel what you know in your heart.
Don't put words on it.
Don't try to capture it.
Let it BECOME you.
You are its vessel.

I am standing around the Chalice Well in Avalon, the site of the Mary ley line and the Red Spring. Her waters flow with the iron oxide of our blood. The Magdalene is here with us in Her full force of love.

There are twenty of us—priestess sisters—who have been traveling through eons to be here now.

We begin a simple, profoundly life changing ceremony to choose love.

This is the sole purpose of our being together.

As each sister speaks the words "I choose love," I feel them as visceral vibrational mantras being sent out across the collective web that we are all woven into.

I feel it touching all those who are choosing hate, all those who are choosing judgment, all those who are choosing to stay asleep.

I feel this energy touching all of the places across our ravaged world where love is most needed. I see all the world leaders who are lost in the chaos being permeated and immersed in this love.

Not love as platitude; not fuzzy and warm, cozy and easy.

A love, as it turns out, that is deeply confronting, challenging, demanding ... a force to be reckoned with.

As women, we are being called into a kind of evolutionary Divine Feminine leadership where we embody love, breathing in the fire of the hate and separation—and choosing to be stellar alchemists who transmute this hate into the elixir of our collective awakening.

This asks us to witness what we've been blindly unconscious to and become willing to *consciously* choose what has held us separate ... where we fall short of love.

So instead of judging, we return to love.

Every day I stumble and see more clearly when I am choosing to turn away from my heart—even just little bit.

And every day I am called to breathe that in and choose love again ... first for myself and then for the other, knowing that in the end, there is no difference.

That is what it means to walk through the gateway of choosing love.

I am being asked to take the apparent risk and surrender to the truth of who I truly am.

This gateway belongs to all of us and I am standing at its door with you, sweetheart.

I am standing, shaking.

Will you choose love with me?

Elayne Kalila Doughty, MA, MFT, has been on the path of passionate service for the past twenty years. She is an ordained Priestess and the founder of the Priestess Presence Temple—a dedicated temple of the 13 Moon Mystery School which initiates women into the ancient mysteries of the Divine Feminine—in a modern context. Through embodiment practices and devoted service, the temple inspires women to unleash their leadership gifts and step into their full potential. Elayne specializes in helping  women tap into their deepest wisdom, enabling them to harness their own transformational power to be more effective and whole in every aspect of their lives. She is a psychotherapist and a global, social, and spiritual activist (see www.globalgratitudealliance.org—the organization she co-founded), best-selling author, speaker, and soul midwife. You can connect with Elayne at **www.priestesspresence.com.**

For the one who sang me into being ...
my own Great Mother, Becky
~Aurora

She Who Holds

BY AURORA FARBER

She's here.
Lying in my arms …
I can't believe it.
She's here!
My child, so wanted, so loved.
My child, so perfect, so fragile, so new.
My child miraculously made in my body
By simply following the rhythm of my womb's wisdom.
I am stretched beyond imagination.
This birth, the starting point of my own evolution,
Cracking my heart open,
burning love flooding my entire body.
In this first embrace
I am reborn as Mother.
I am She Who Holds.

My evolution was induced the day I decided to have a child—as a sacred intention to birth something new. This wild idea that I could do something that I didn't really "know" how to do. And yet, I did. Formed within my own body temple, a miracle unfolded in the shape of a child.

Motherhood has been my path of transformation, each child singing my evolution forward. Lullabies of welcome, others of sorrow, others of possibility. Each child and their song ushering my own birth into someone I could never have imagined.

I always wanted to be a mother. Except for morning sickness, my first pregnancy was magical. Each day I felt a little jewel growing inside me … how blessed I was to become a mother, especially for the first time at age thirty-five.

At twenty weeks I found out she was a girl—exactly as I had hoped. Years before, I had already named her while on a boat in Turkey. Drifting on a river between the East and West, Europe and Asia, I named her Aja Soleil, meaning *Eastern Sun*. I wrote her name in my journal and wrote to her as though she were with me already. In my twenties and thirties, I continued to journal to her as I navigated the seas of my own becoming.

Our dialogue, started years before, continued while she was in my womb. One day, her song came through me …

The sun and the moon
The stars and the skies
All are reflected in your loving eyes.
Whole and complete
A gift from above.
We surround you with our love.
Aja Soleil, Aja Soleil
Hey-eh-eh, Eh eh eh, Eh.
Like the "eastern sun"
glowing warm and bright
You bring us hope, joy and light.

This was her welcome song. Aja Soleil—a rising sun, so loved and wanted. This was my welcome song, too: a mother—whole and complete, filled with hope, joy and light.

With a full heart and my arms gently holding this miracle I had called into being, I sang to her.

She Who Is Held
I'm spinning in a burgundy void
What started as life has ended.
Longing to meet you
You are gone…

Just. Like. That.
I'll never hold you in my arms.
Never see your beautiful eyes
Or feel your soft skin
Never know the scent of you…
And yet I know you are all around me.
In the vast sky above
In the earth below
You've changed me.
Heart broken open in grief
The ground beneath me spinning
I long to hold you
I long to be held.
I am She Who Is Held.

I never got to hold my precious second baby, the child I "mis-carried." She fell away from me and cracked me open like a burst of lightning in the sky. We named her Emmanuelle Tian. Emmanuelle means "God among us" and Tian means "sky" in Mandarin Chinese.

I still call her Elle. *Elle, my angel in the sky.* The one I longed to hold, the one who showed me that I needed to be held.

We had been living in Shanghai, China when I got pregnant. It was perfect timing since we were at the end of our six-month contract. I went back to my hometown in the United States, feeling happy that I would have this child with my family nearby.

Thrilled to be pregnant again, I went to the OB/GYN and heard the sweet sounds of her heartbeat. Leaving the office, I proudly carried the ultrasound, her first photo. I told my extended family and a few friends. We couldn't wait to welcome her home.

But that would never happen. One day I started to bleed. Something was happening and I couldn't stop it. At the doctor's office it was confirmed. No heartbeat. My baby was gone.

The days afterward were a blur. *I consciously chose to grieve this loss, to create a sacred space in my life to feel her presence, even if it was terribly painful.* But how? I had so little to hold onto. A simple black and white ultrasound? A pregnancy stick? I needed something of her to hold. Only then I could finally let her go.

My grief was boundless. I wondered if it would ever end. To mark the passage of time, I decided to teach myself to knit. It was a meditation, a dedication to the child I would never hold. Each stitch an embrace, until finally I made a tiny, blue baby blanket to hold my broken heart.

My family wanted to help me but didn't know how. I struggled with closure, trying to end something that had barely begun. My grief felt private and personal. How could anyone understand? I could feel her all around me, knowing her passing and her presence were part of my own evolution as a mother. Knowing somehow that this initiation into the darkness was actually *for* me, I finally understood that "Mother" is not only she who holds, but She Who Is Held.

The grief finally became too much for me to bear alone. Broken, I asked for what my soul needed to move from grief to acceptance. I needed the short life and endless gift of sweet Emmanuelle to be witnessed. I needed for those who loved me to hold me so I could finally say goodbye.

I asked my family to meet on the beach at dusk and created a ceremony of farewell for my child. As each family member read their passages, tears of welcome and release streamed down my face like the ebb and flow of the ocean before me. These sacred words became Elle's lullaby, sung by my family to heal my soul.

Brother: *Today we come together in sorrow over the death of Aurora and Rhett's baby. Their child, created in love and eagerly wished for, has died—never to be nestled securely in their arms in this lifetime. To these parents, the pain and the disappointment are great, and their loss will be carried heavily in their hearts in the weeks and months ahead. They will miss their child terribly and will be in need of love, compassion, time and understanding from all of us.*

Sister-in-law: *Each life comes into this world with a mission. Sometimes the mission or purpose is clear; sometimes it is vague and shrouded in misunderstandings. In time, we will see what this baby's mission was on earth. Could it have been just to add a little flicker of love that otherwise may never have been lit? Was it to soften our hearts so that we may in turn comfort others? Could it have been to bring us closer to God and to each other?*

Husband: *This child's life was short, yet the death has left a huge void in all of our hearts and lives. Let us remember today and for always the tiny baby who will never see childhood or adulthood but will remain our tiny baby, our tiny angel forever.*

Father: *What name have you given this child?*

My husband and I: *Emmanuelle Tian*

Mother: *We bathe this child in the love of God. We bathe this child in the tears of her parents and family. We know the power of water to permeate life and hold this child. The water of the womb sustained this child as the water of the universe and the power of God will hold this tiny baby now and for eternity.*

Me: *He who created you … He who formed you … fear not, for I have redeemed you. I have summoned you by name; you are mine.*
—*Isaiah 43:1*

With the ocean waves rolling behind me, I became She Who Is Held. Held by love, held by family, held by an angel that I could always find in the sky.

She Who Ignites the Spark
Rolling and rocking
In an ocean of possibilities
I feel your rhythm.
Alive with hope again,
My body hums a new song.
There's something gentle about you
Something strong and constant, yet fiery.
My heart, on fire with love for you,
As the song of you completes me.

A whispered prayer of hope
Is how you came to be
Now you're here so strong and brave
For all of the world to see.

Stars from the heavens shine down on you
Your heart glows from within
With courage and strength and wisdom's truth
Faith is where love begins ...

A mother's love, A father's pride,
So grand you are to see.
A sister's joy, Sweet baby boy,
You've blessed our family.
I am She Who Ignites The Spark

My last child completed our family in so many ways. I still remember his first flutterings and how they made my heart sing. We named him Rhys, which means "fiery and enthusiastic" and Alexander, "protector of mankind." A powerful name to carry. Little did I know that his fiery soul would light a fire in me.

He was born in Shanghai, and by this time, I had been practicing the gifts of a mother who holds *and* is held. We hired a full-time maid who became a second mother to him and a dear helpmate and companion for me. She took care of the house and, when needed, cooked and babysat for us. Because I had so much support, I was able to pursue my own interests and passions. I discovered painting and Chinese Medicine. I worked out and studied Mandarin. I taught Pilates and learned pole dancing. I worked with local and international parents and founded our school's first PTA. I joined and created circles of women for sisterhood: a moms' group, a book club, a Kindermusik group for moms and babies. I ran workshops on creating extraordinary families and magical marriages.

My son's curiosity about the world mirrored my own. I now felt more balanced in the way I mothered—less worried, more adventurous, like him. I felt supported because I could delegate tasks and have time to "mother" my own dreams. I began to ask myself, "What more do I want to do with my life?"

I decided to become a Feminine Leadership Coach and discovered an online program of study. I fell in love with coaching and the magic that happens by co-creating a relationship with a client. Above all, I created my own schedule and had plenty of time for my family.

My son's birth lit the masculine in me. The part that wanted to do more than mother my children. The part that wanted to make a difference in the world. The part that wanted to claim my "Mythic Self" who was Mother— but also so much more.

I had been steeped in the feminine world of mothering for so long and, though I loved it, I yearned for more. I saw my son's energy, his enthusiasm and desire to explore, and I wanted that, too. Finally, my own inner marriage of masculine and feminine came into balance so I could pursue my sacred work outside of family.

She Who Tends the Flame
I'm falling, falling, falling
Is there no end?
Why me?
So scared,
So alone.
I don't want to die.
It's so cold, so dark here,
Only the moon to guide me.
I will surrender
Let go.
I feel an inner flame
Expanding my heart.
I breathe it in …
Power.
Love.
Wisdom.
I remember
I am She Who Tends the Flame.

After almost ten years in China, we decided to leave. For years, I'd wanted to move back to the United States, but my husband wanted to stay. Finally the chance to leave … and I held back. However, due to a variety of circumstances such as pollution and the economy, we knew when it was ultimately time to go home.

We were only back home for about a week when I fell into depression. I missed our old life, our friends, the places we used to go. I thought coming back to my hometown would be easy, familiar … but it had changed. I had changed. I wondered if moving "home" had been the right choice.

With so much to do in starting our new life, I pushed these feelings aside. I made sure everyone else was adjusting and ignored the signs of my own depression. Like moms everywhere, I shopped, cooked, cleaned, mended bruises and fragile hearts. I missed our maid and thought nostalgically about the gift her service gave to our family—especially to me.

Things finally began to settle until the day I got a call from my dermatologist and heard those dreaded words.

"Your biopsy came back positive."

I was diagnosed with melanoma, a very scary and dangerous type of skin cancer. It was caught early and removed, but the *fear* of cancer could not be extracted with the surgery.

I became even more depressed. Lethargic and fearful of going out in the sun, I retreated from the world and sought the sanctuary of home. Months passed and I continued to hibernate, fearing to hope for too much, wanting only to be safe. Doctors terrified me with horrible cancer stories. I was afraid of the sun and covered myself from head to toe.

I felt nothing. Numb with despair, I was empty, flat, lifeless. I was held prisoner of my own fear. The darkness enveloped me until I knew I couldn't continue to go on like this.

Finally at my breaking point, I surrendered. I let go.

Instead of running away from these painful feelings of fear and despair, I choose to turn toward them. I began by creating a morning ritual. Each day I lit a candle, hoping it would light something in me again. I sat in silence and prayed. I took long, candle-lit baths where I meditated and then anointed my body with essential oils. I drew oracle cards and created an altar that I changed and tended daily. I began to adore and adorn my body as though it were a sacred vessel, choosing scents and clothing for the woman I hoped to become again.

Still fearful of the sun, I marked the slow passage of time by watching the moon. Night time became "my time," and one night while sitting in my garden, I noticed the tiny, white sliver of the moon winking at me. Fascinated, I sat a nightly vigil watching the moon blossom into a bright and radiant orb, only to shrink into the darkness again.

I was mesmerized, captivated. Hope had found its way to my heart again. If the changing moon could blossom into fullness, maybe I could, too.

The moon became a guide to my own internal rhythm. I began to count time in cycles instead of months, knowing that in each moon cycle there was a time to be full and out in the world and a time to be empty, to nestle into oneself, in order to bloom again.

I created my first moon journal and on the cover I placed a collage of my one desire—to find joy again. Each new moon became a time to release old stories and set new intentions. Each full moon was a time to celebrate the blessings in life.

Each day these intentional practices fanned my inner heart flame—the triple flame of power, love, and wisdom. In the darkness, I lit my own feminine fire and, by tending to it daily, I grew stronger and learned to love myself again and to listen to my inner wisdom. The fire of my own transformation burned away my limiting beliefs, helping me align once again to my purpose and passion. My body, a temple of my own evolution, made sacred by tending the flame.

She Who Stands In The Fire

I am here now
Pregnant, this time,
With possibility.
A new world awaits
Feminine energy rising
Swirling, expanding
The old system crumbling
A world in chaos.
From the ashes
A new song of sisterhood arises
A remembrance of our
Power
Love
Wisdom.
A fire now lit in our hearts
Flaming through our bodies
Alchemizing all into love.
Sisters everywhere,

Burning down all that no longer serves,
Birthing a new paradigm.
Together we forge a new world,
A world ablaze with feminine fire.
I am She Who Stands in the Fire.

Today, I stand with other women, heralding the birth of the New Feminine Evolutionary. We are each creating something new, something unimaginable, something crafted in passion, and held in love—like a child forming in the womb. Birthing this new being, we birth ourselves into being.

Each of us comes onto the path of feminine evolution differently. Motherhood has been my path, destroying illusions of who I think I am and reconstructing something new from the ashes each day. It surprises me, exhausts me, thrills me. It wears me out and builds me up again, evolving me into a stronger, more loving and wiser woman.

The New Feminine Evolutionary inside all of us is waiting to be born, needing to be born. Our world is crumbling; old structures and traditions failing with the patriarchy fighting desperately for power once more.

Our earth is crying, our children ravaged by war and disease, our brothers and sisters lost and afraid. We need a guide, a light to ignite the spark of hope again, a melody to lead us through the dark night into the light of day.

Something stirs in the darkness. Like the lullabies that called my children into being, I hear a new birthing song.

A song of hope. A song of sisters rising. A song of sisters reaching in to reach out and heal the world. A song of the heart, reminding us of our own innate power, love, and wisdom. A sacred song, guiding us from transition to crowning, until at last, we marvel at our own evolution, cradled gently in our arms. A song birthing the New Feminine Evolutionary into being.

I am She Who Holds.
I am She Who Is Held.
I am She Who Ignites the Spark.
I am She Who Tends the Flame.
I am She Who Stands In the Fire.
I am She.

Aurora Anurca Farber, *Transforma-*
tional Coach, Writer, and International
Speaker and Relationship Educator, is
on a mission to help women ignite their
"Feminine Fire" (the heart-light within
that integrates life-giving power, com-
passionate love and intuitive wisdom).
These three feminine flames are the key
to catalyzing passionate and purposeful
action that will heal our world. Becoming
a mother deepened Aurora's appreciation
of women as life-givers and caretakers.
She believes that every woman is a sacred
vessel, and by integrating our three feminine power centers of womb, heart and
mind, we become portals of unlimited creation ... whether that is creating a
child in the womb, an inspiring business, or a thriving community! Aurora's
own creations include programs that help women connect to intentional, plea-
surable and purposeful living. Her signature program, "I Am SHE: Awaken the
Feminine Evolutionary Within", supports women as they activate the archetype
of the Feminine Evolutionary and claim their sacred work and divine purpose.
Aurora holds honors degrees in Literature and Foreign Language, along with
a professional certification in Coaching. She has been a featured speaker and
relationship workshop facilitator in Hong Kong, Malaysia, Taiwan, China and
the US. She loves exploring the world and has been to over forty countries and
lived in Europe and Asia most of her adult life. Her most recent travel adven-
ture can be found at www.TheExtraordinaryFamilyAdventure.com, a travel and
relationship blog exploring "sacred spaces" in relationship and nature. This for-
ty-day family odyssey through the Western United States inspired the creation
of, "The Family Compass: 4 Keys to Creating Your Own Extraordinary Fam-
ily," a relationship training program focusing on the power of "Vision, Clarity,
Connection and Ritual" to create intentional, sacred relationships. Through
private coaching, online programs, women's circles and retreats, Aurora creates
"sacred spaces" for women to be held, witnessed and loved exactly as they are
right here, right now. Her guiding vision is a world of women claiming their
creative powers, loving their body temples, and being beacons of fierce wisdom
as they burn away archaic, limiting beliefs and light the world on fire with love.
Learn more: ***www.aurorafarber.com***

Let My Rivers Flow

BY WHITNEY FREYA

These words flowed through me while spending personal retreat time immersed in the sacred land of my home in Oregon. I offer them as a prayer and invite you to read it aloud. As you speak these words into the ethers, you expand this evolutionary woman energy across our magical and beautiful planet, infusing all sentient beings with a spark of light and awareness. Thank you for choosing to BE the change.

As an evolutionary woman, I now understand that life right now is like waking up from a long dream. I can see clearly now that I've now woken up and remembered the truth of who I am. I AM an evolutionary woman, a healer, a priestess, a way-shower, a guide, a magician, a midwife, a poet, an artist, a dancer, a mother, a sustainer, a nurturer. I AM Gaia. I AM a beautiful landscape of rivers and valleys, of waterfalls, of light, of shadowy spaces and illuminated places.

I remember now that Mother Gaia longs to reconnect with me, after my long slumber, to remind me that she and I are one, that our journey back to wholeness, to reclaim our own wilderness, to be able to radiate and shine our true nature, is our shared journey. For both of us have been raped, pillaged, extorted, violated, suppressed, controlled, fenced in, damned, burned, and killed.

Now, at this point of awakening, I remember union, I remember that all the answers that I seek lie within me and You, both with the humus of our physical body, our energetic body, and our Mother Earth body. Whatever we need to keep the air clean, to drink from pristine waters, to sustain life beneath the surface of the ocean and life on the plains, in the mountains and jungles ... is what you need, what I need, to thrive. Whatever the land needs to harvest bountiful harvests, sustain our human family and flourish, is what you need, what I need, to manifest that which we came here to create. We simply need to look back to the source, to the way our true nature already does those things.

Somewhere, I forgot how to be wild and free. Alongside, Mother Gaia was also stripped of her wild fenced in and drilled into, paved over and mined, her wild spaces tamed and exploited. How has her journey mirrored my own?

As an evolutionary woman, I now understand my journey in this lifetime is to live my truest nature and to wake up from the stories that have kept me small, that have made me feel weaker, less than, or not as worthy. I relinquish the ways I have allowed myself to be at the mercy of something bigger, to be fearful. I now remember the vastness of my web, as Grandmother Spider, I remember the interconnected nature of *all things*. I AM evolutionary woman. When Mother Gaia and I reunite we will lead humanity into a new birth. We are the birthers of worlds.

Gaia, the Goddess, the divine feminine, the evolutionary woman ... I remember union as I take back my own wildness, as I uproot the stakes that have attempted to fence me in, to keep my ideas safe and small and ... powerless. As I blast away the dams that have blocked my creative flow, as I take back my voice and choose to once again thunder and rumble and shake the structures that have been built, that have not been aligned with nature, I will reclaim my sovereignty and my power. Anything that exploits, destroys, or pollutes Mother Earth does the same to me. Just as Mother Earth creates and grows and manifests from within, so I, as evolutionary woman, will lead humanity to a new earth.

With these words, I activate a knowing deep within me. The reason I have been made to feel less than is because, in truth, I am *all*. The truth behind the suppression, the control, the discrimination is that I, as evolutionary woman, AM the change. The logical, the rational, the masculine fears change. I will help them conquer their fears as I conquer my own. As I weave my world into alignment with my heart, I will create a tapestry of new beginnings.

I understand now that the earth-based stories, the folklore, the myths, the fairy tales have all been symbolic of the truth. The earth-based stories of my childhood will guide me back to my innocence, before I knew anything other than truth.

I choose to connect now to Grandmother Spider or Spider Woman, the weaver of worlds, the Mother of the Universe. I understand now that it is her story that guides us back to the truth that any scientist would be able to prove: that life energy, the fabric of our existence, our union with Mother Earth and our individual lives is exactly like a spider web, interconnected and acutely sensitive so that whenever anything happens in any part of the web, it is felt throughout. We are one. Separation is an illusion. This spider web and the stories of Grandmother Spider remind me of this very real truth.

Likewise, the trees root themselves deep into Mother Earth as well as grow and reach to the light. Rivers flow and keep life fresh, watered, nourished, and sustained until they are dammed or blocked, or polluted. If a river is straightened to make room for roads and agriculture, the water table goes down, the wildlife dwindles, and life diminishes. Curves are power.

I choose to connect to the energy of the river now. I understand the truth of the ways the wild waters have been tamed, dammed, eroded, and polluted. Now, I understand that I have shared the experience. I entered this world overflowing with enthusiasm and singing my own song. But, I, too was tamed, dammed, and polluted.

My mother's generation tried to fit into suits and "slacks." The corner office was the finish line. She tried to be man. Now, I understand that what is needed universally, within and without, is more curves, more nature, more truth, more wildness … less order, fewer partitions and boundaries and borders and barricades. Fewer rules and more receptivity will be the pathway back to balance and harmony.

My own true nature is meant to flow freely down its natural channels, and it has been blocked by naysayers, by logic, by the rational mind, by fear, the desire or belief in security and safety.

Let my rivers flow.

Let my rivers flow clear.

If they become blocked, dammed, or polluted, I am only blocking, damming, or polluting my own desires, my own everything. Everything on Mother Earth echoes her love and are the keys to my survival.

As an evolutionary woman, I understand that remembering this union, creating a new intimate relationship with Gaia, remembering the wild crafts, the ancient modes of healing, seeking out spaces and places where I can feel the pulse of my heart, the pulse of the bird call, the wind, the babbling brooks, is the medicine I bring to my world. I choose to bring it now as an evolutionary woman.

I AM evolutionary woman. I AM Gaia. I am waking up to remember that I have always been merged with her. I can now weave my awareness, my consciousness into the land around me. The butterfly's flight reminds me to be light and playful. The flowers remind me to grow toward the light. The breeze whispers greetings from my brothers and sisters all around the world, and each blade of grass celebrates the light, the rain, and the air.

Evolutionary woman, welcome home. Welcome home to your own wilderness. I lend you my strength, the energy of my mountains, the power of my rivers, the boundlessness of my oceans to help you reconnect to who you truly are and to grow and manifest that which has been planted deepest in your heart. Reach toward the light and understand that as you do, so everyone else will follow, like ripples in a still pond caused by a single, small pebble.

As life and our world becomes that much more complicated and intense, I now understand the respite and the guidance the land around me, Gaia, has to offer. I know that you have available to you the truest wisdom, just outside your door. Personally, with all the changes I have experienced over the past five years, becoming un-married, raising three teens, and growing my soul-led business, I cannot imagine handling it all without my frequent voyages into Gaia, even if just a short walk to a special tree. Imagine that the land wants to bathe you in love and truth. Treat yourself to this energy as much as you can, evolutionary woman. Weave your being into the land. As you do, feel your truth, your wild nature, expand and free itself. I honor you and your journey, as we all share in your ebbs and flows.

A'Ho.

Whitney Freya has been facilitating creative learning since 1996 when she opened The Creative Fitness Center. Since then, she has traveled globally as a creativity expert, published three books on personal creativity, including her latest book published by Flower of Life Press, Rise Above, Free Your Mind One Brushstroke at a Time, *and founded her Creatively Fit Coaching Certification Program to ensure as many people as possible remember their infinite creative nature in as supportive a way as possible. She has*

facilitated her process at The Esalen Institute, Burning Man, The Agape Spiritual Center, and creativity conferences in South Africa, Dubai, Canada and the United States. She has appeared on summits alongside Dr. Wayne Dyer, Donna Eden and more. Humanitarian News recognized Whitney for her work with Women for Women International. She lives in the "wild west" of Northeast Oregon with her three teenagers, who LOVE to "think creatively!" Learn more and connect at **WhitneyFreya.com.**

Embodied Essence

BY ANAHITA JOON

MOMENT OF DOUBT

I wonder what I can possibly write worthy of these critical times in which we find ourselves. The human family is tasked with going beyond our fears of scarcity and separation. Individuals, as well as the collective, are forced to face the unconscious shadow on the path to wholeness. Our planet is diminishing in her vitality.

Write what you know; write who you are, she says.

"But the journey has been so messy and it has taken so long to put the pieces together to see clearly," I protest. "I am not perfect. There have been so many wounds."

NO! You are my masterpiece, she echoes in my being.

A dam of tears—tears that I didn't know existed—breaks, and I allow myself a breath of relief. "What if it's not enough?" I plead.

What if it is? She doesn't miss a beat. *I have placed the seed of each of you within the others. You will find each other. Those wounds were your rights of passage. Tell them the story of the wild woman who could not be contained. Trust me!*

"Yes, find each other," I breathe a little deeper. "Yes, I remember why I am here."

This resounding unconditionally loving voice has been the true and, often, fierce beacon of love guiding my way for the past sixteen years.

At first, I had no name for her. She is Mother, Goddess, an all-encompassing love, and the greatest space of permission I have ever known. She has led me through the darkest corners of my being I never would have otherwise had the courage to face, ultimately landing me in almost unimaginable freedom.

> *I give thanks as the light of the Goddess and the wisdom of the*
> *enchanted feminine spirit run through me, and as me, for the*
> *betterment of all.*

It's 4:30 a.m. and I'm driving on the Pacific Coast Highway to open the coffee shop where I work from 5:30 until noon, before heading to the office to work for a spiritual counselor. It doesn't feel like morning outside, but it does in my soul. Outside it is still dark and the full moon is shimmering over the ocean. My life feels like it is finally mine. I feel myself settling into a new way of being in the world as these words pour in from the top of my head.

> *I give thanks as the light of the Goddess and the wisdom of the*
> *enchanted feminine spirit run through me, and as me, for the*
> *betterment of all.*

I'm not sure how exactly, but these words take root instantly and become the resonating soundtrack of my inner being. *YES!* my soul is screaming, *I am all in, use me, make art of my life that it may serve the greater good!* My mind has no idea how I am to be used, just that I am a YES.

I once heard a preacher say, "God wants to know if the answer is YES. What you are saying YES to is none of your business." It's true, I had no idea what I would be saying YES to other than my own aliveness, but, quite frankly, that was enough. I would spend two years in total surrender to this guidance. She commands and I say YES.

Stop eating meat and other animals.
"Okay," I say.
Use your last $400 to go Washington, D.C., to lobby for a peace bill.
"Okay," I say.
Leave your job and sell your things to move to D.C.
"Okay," I say.
Dance, she says.
I say, "Okay."

AM I STILL ALIVE?

The year is 1986 and Iran and Iraq are at war. I am seven years old, and the bombs going off are the norm. In fact, they have been going off my whole life. The radio is the fastest way to know if there is a threat of bombs being dropped, so it is always on in the background, even at school during class and at night when we sleep at home.

The sirens vary in intensity to indicate how soon the bombs will hit. The sound of a yellow siren indicates we may have up to five minutes to take cover, orange indicates three minutes, and red means about one minute to find shelter before a bomb is dropped. At which point, I close my eyes, hold my breath and my father's hand, and wait for the *BOOM*. The earth shakes and I open my eyes. *Am I still alive?*

Fear is everywhere. I am a child of the revolution. I cannot wear shorts or a miniskirt or feel the sunlight on my legs in any way. As I step outside to streets covered with military police and their guns, I wonder about a time when women and men could socialize freely.

I had heard of a time when a woman could sing freely. Today, in my seven-year-old world, the sound of a woman's song is illegal. Apparently, the song of a woman is too seductive and, therefore, a sin if heard by men outside her immediate family.

I have seen what oppression can do to men and women.

I have seen staggering numbers of perfectly intelligent women lose their sanity and break down.

I have known women who, in trying to get a divorce in Iran, were forced to sleep with the government officials in charge of granting their divorce.

I have seen men become soldiers of hate, greed, fear, and separation.

Body of skin, of moss, of eager and firm milk.
Oh the goblets of the breast!
Oh the eyes of absence!
Oh the roses of the pubis!

~Pablo Neruda

LIBERATION'S DOOR

I have always had a fascination with strip clubs, a deep curiosity. I knew these places had a secret, and I needed to be let in. At first, being a waitress was a safe way to explore my curiosity. That is until Red, who changed everything and gave me the courage to live my destiny.

Red is my best friend, a true soul sister. Ours is the kind of friendship you know from the first moment will go on forever. I love her deeply and we are seekers together. We both have jobs, the non-strip club kind. We both volunteer and spend time studying spiritual texts and attending meditation retreats. Also, we drink lots of tequila—it's our thing. After all, we are twenty-two-year-olds living in Los Angeles.

One night, sitting at the foot of my four-poster bed, I am talking to Red and telling her about the women at the club where I waitress. The truth is I envy the women who dance. They have a freedom I cannot imagine as my own. This is beyond frightening.

In my attempt to cope with this fear, I create the perfect separation in my mind. "Naturally," I tell Red, "we are different. I am a good girl, I am educated, I come from an educated family, I am an activist. I am not like them. They are outcasts and probably have no family and live in the shadows of society. So, there you have it. We are obviously different."

My opinions about the strippers must have been teetering on blatant judgment, because, out of what seems like nowhere, Red says, "Listen, I need you to stop talking shit about strippers."

"Why is that?" I ask.

"Because I am one!" she tells me.

"What? No, you are not, you are like me. You are a good girl, we are virtuous and smart, and we do good things in the world."

Once the initial shock wears off, she invites me to come watch her dance. Watching Red dance is the beginning of what would become the undoing of my perfectly built cage.

The club is right on the famous Sunset Strip. I am sitting at the edge of a large stage as the red strobe lights dance on the blank canvas of the stage floor. It's Friday night, and men and women fill the house, ready to be entertained, inspired, turned on, or all of the above.

Red takes the floor with grace and confidence as the DJ announces her name. She wears little red shorts, black boots and her red hair in pigtails. She climbs to the top of the pole and drops into the splits. She takes her hair out, shakes it off and starts to crawl toward the audience, and then me. She is having such a good time.

This is the moment my identity begins to deconstruct.

Wait! ... Is that available? I didn't know that was on the menu! For a good girl, that is, a girl like me.

While I am nowhere near ready to dance like Red, nor at the time do I think I ever will be, this moment changes everything. I am now set on a path of dismantling every belief handed down to me by religion, country, father, and society as I come face to face with the feminine face of God.

We all have these beings who come into our lives and initiate us into the greater truths of our soul and give us permission to be more of who we are. Red is my agent of freedom.

ECSTASY—I AM THE TEMPLE

Two years have passed and I find myself at another strip club. This time I am in Washington, D.C., and this time I am dancing. I am here because this wisdom that has been powerfully guiding me for two years is telling me to say YES.

You will dance and you will send the freedom back to your ancestors and all women who are oppressed in the Middle East.

"Okay," I say.

Backstage, I get a fair amount of grief from the women. I find myself repeatedly criticized for being happy, for smiling, for enjoying myself, and am labeled as phony and inauthentic.

A lot of the women here are exchanging their sexual energy for money because they feel trapped.

But I am having the time of my life. Coming from a culture so heavily informed by oppression, specifically of female sensual/sexual energies, you bet I am happy and enjoying myself. The young woman who once feared the liberation she witnessed in other women has now become a full-blown sensual dancer, transmuting the static and mundane into blissful ecstasy for herself and others.

It is Friday night, and men and women of all ages pack the club. The pulse of the hip-hop music nearly shakes the building as I approach the stage. I hear my song, something slow and sexy. I glide slowly onto the dance space and begin to go into an ecstatic state as my clothes come off, piece by piece. My dress is not simply a dress, but the shackles of a thousand years. As the lace of my dress falls to my feet, the doors to an ultimate freedom open in my soul.

By the time I am down to my bottoms and pasties, I have a huge smile on my face and am in full communion with the Divine. My primal essence is dancing me. It's not uncommon that I look down and see a man sitting at my stage with his hands interlocked as he leans onto his elbows. He looks like he is praying and that is perfectly fine with me. He, like many others, is among the most powerful in the nation's capital and he has come to pray.

I AM the temple.

I catch his eyes as I fall into a back bend, my heart is lifting, my back arched, my breath gasping. He looks relieved as he smiles. There is a space of deep permission that lives between us. My heart feels bigger for allowing him to see me in my ecstasy and his armor seems to be falling off, piece by piece. We both know I am not really dancing for him, but simply allowing him to witness me.

Here, we are allowed our primal essence, our desires, our hunger, our lust. It is this primal desire and key to our aliveness that perpetuates our species. Yet, we are so fully bought into the shame set forth by patriarchy that our source of life has become commoditized, tucked into the shadows, and shamed.

WOLF MEDICINE AND THE PATRIARCHY

"Patriarchy: The fear of lack, scarcity, which is sourced in the mind and perpetuates separation, including the ego-based agendas that are formed by the ego's fear of loss and death."

~Anahita Joon

I have been working for a self-proclaimed guru from India. He had the endorsement of some big names in the integral and holistic fields when I came on board. Since then, he has lost the endorsements. We are working day and night, putting in an average of ninety hours a week. The goal is to get as many people to receive blessings as possible. These "blessings" are done remotely or in person and are grossing the business over half a million dollars per quarter. It has become incredibly clear to me this man is not interested in service. But I can't break free. I am too deep in the patriarchy, and my power feels far away. This organization is running on fear, scarcity, and separation, and so am I.

I feel like I am having an acid flashback, except I haven't done acid. The decorative masks on my wall in my room are staring at me. I take them down and shove them under the bed. I sit down to catch my breath, but it's not slowing down. Whatever is happening is happening now. My memory bank pulls from my studies with the Ecuadorian shaman and I realize I am about to cross the boundaries of human form. I put on some drum music and burn a stick of sage. I am scared.

The air looks different. I try to steady my feet, but I lose the battle and drop to my knees on the Persian carpet covering my apartment floor. *Oh, my Goddess, I am turning into a wild animal*, is my last cognitive thought as my crawling intensifies and I become a wild growling creature. The wild animal raises her head. I try to catch myself in the floor mirror, but I am not there. She is all wolf and, growling with the curled back lips unique to wolves, she begins transmitting a message to me. It would take me seven years to fully decode the message. She leaves as I melt on to the floor and curl into the fetal position.

I carry the message of the wolf for seven years before I know what it means. She didn't have words like *anger* or *rage*, but simply growled because energetic and ethical boundaries were being crossed while I stayed at my job. She was an expression of my power in the face of the patriarchy's deep claws into my life and psyche. Through her, my primal essence bypassed my mind, which was infected by the poison of fear and separation imbued by the patriarchy. Through the alchemy of expressing her energy, I was able to leave my position with the guru, let go of fear, and restore my integrity.

When I speak of patriarchy, I am not speaking of the association with only men but rather the current systems created to support the rise of man and the silencing of woman. Patriarchy is a system whose goal has been nothing short of the full extinction of the voice of the deep feminine living in all women and men. I am not interested in talking about the patriarchy being wrong, simply the truth: It is killing us. It is killing us by shaming the very thing that makes us alive, our primal essence.

Have you ever seen a wild animal be ashamed of its mating rituals? Of course not. We are the only animals who live with and experience shame around our sexuality, lust, desire, and hunger. We are also the only animals destroying our natural habitat that sustains us. A civilization that is alive and in sync with the pulse of its planet will not rape and pillage the earth and her people. It is the deep wounds of self-hatred and shame that do that. I have learned this shame extends to our anger and rage and, ultimately, any expression of our primal essence.

Don't be afraid of your primal essence. If you are afraid to get angry, and I mean really angry, examine your fear. Have a look at our world. Do you see boundaries being crossed? Release your concern of not wanting to be an angry woman and dive deeply into the bloody heart of your rage. It is in the moment of granting permission to be the rage that the alchemy occurs and you can claim the surge of anger in your body to be power.

This choice and power of alchemy is what sets us apart from other animals, and ultimately what makes it safe for us to harness the power of our primal essence. This ability to choose is what makes it safe for you to explore the edge of your sexuality, your lust, your desire, without becoming a savage animal.

WEAVING A TAPESTRY OF FREEDOM

Within the design of patriarchy, our primary relationship with female sexuality and our earth have been to possess and commoditize. The day we can stop this relationship is the day we free ourselves from oppression.

So how do we get there? It is only when the body of woman and the body of the earth can be recognized as one life-giving force and held in reverence that we may have an opportunity to create a harmonious existence. For woman, it begins with questioning everything and rewriting the narrative around her sexuality, her passion, her desire, and even her rage. Everything must be questioned: every belief, every doubt, every fear, and stitch of shame.

Woman is life. She is the temple. As she recognizes her body as the body of our mother Gaia, she is restored in her life-giving and life-affirming powers. She must learn how to listen and honor her own sense of aliveness over the fears of scarcity and separation, handed down to her by a system designed exclusively to squelch her true power. These fears are designed to perpetuate a world that no longer works and whose destruction is ensured if the current system is not dismantled.

Woman, you are the answer.

If you are a woman reading this, please do what it takes to free yourself, for we are one body. You, me, and the young women enslaved around the world are of one flesh. To be blessed with the opportunity of Western freedom comes with great responsibility. Let us not seek position within the current design, but trust our own sense of aliveness to lead the way. Let us do what is required to raise the bar of possibility for woman, for Earth, and for humanity.

We must all learn how to put our aliveness before our ego's agenda. Man, too, needs to learn how to be in a new relationship with his own primal desires. The shift can happen by moving these desires out of the shadows and into the light of unconditional love. Men must remember the source of all life comes from the earth as well as from women. It is critical for men to learn how to receive from the earth's and women's radiance without defaulting to the patriarchal design of wanting to commoditize or possess.

We all need each other. This is a collective healing. There are many women and men who know how to do what I describe here and continue to step forward as teachers. The opportunity lies in not only the gathering of women with women and men with men but also in an education in what it is to witness one another in aliveness.

Contrary to popular belief, this rise of the feminine is not about a higher percentage of female CEOs within the current system. It is, however, about creating a new reality, a sustainable and intelligent system whose design is entirely sourced from the wisdom of our primal bodies, the wisdom of nature herself. It has taken hundreds of years to come into this time in history. In the same manner, this shift is not one to occur overnight. You and I may not live to see the new reality. Can you do what it takes, anyway? When we recognize the intelligence of nature and trust life and death as natural cycles, we unplug from the fear of loss and death. This further allows us to play our integral role in the big picture.

When we push down our desire, lust, and our hunger—which are designed to be a guide to light the path to aliveness—they become a distorted shadow, echoing with shame and self-hatred, thus draining our life force. Let us come away from worshiping at the altar of scarcity and not-enoughness. Let us, instead, be sovereign beings whose lives are a demonstration of resourcefulness, plentifulness, and, most of all, life.

I invite you to commit to cultivating your aliveness as your source of wisdom and legacy. Allow yourself to be seen as one who has come alive. We are all yearning for this, and it has never been safer or more critical to our survival than it is at this moment.

See you on the dance floor!

*Born during the Islamic Revolution of Iran, Anahita's first thirteen years were filled with rich culture, mythical story- telling, living through illness and surviv- ing trauma. As a modern-day priestess, healer, and medicine woman, Anahita has the heart of an ancient Persian mys- tic and power of the serpent. Her work is the culmination of over twenty years of intensive study with mystic masters and shamans, social research, as well as her own teaching. As a Feminine Leader- ship and Empowerment coach, Anahita works with women who are ready to awaken and unleash the force of nature within. Anahita is a credentialed coach and spiritual counselor and creator of The Beautiful Self ™ and Embodied Essence™. Learn more: **www.anahitajoon.com***

Working Through Vulnerability, Fear, and Grief to Claim Inner Power

BY CRISTINA LASKAR

What does power mean to you?

Power, to me, means confidence, authenticity, knowing one's self, open-mindedness, using one's voice, integrity, education (self- or academic), humility, owning who you are, knowing your strengths, admitting your weaknesses, allowing others to support you, and doing the things that make you feel uncomfortable and stretch your edges—maybe even make you a little frozen. Power also means living and acting from your head *and* your heart—connected! Power means love!

I will also share some not so common—and definitely uncomfortable and uncomforting—views of power.

VULNERABILITY

Being vulnerable allows you to just be who you are. It gives others not only permission to do the same but also a feeling of togetherness and oneness. When we share vulnerably and authentically, we are able to see just how similar we all are. However, getting started in the vulnerability game can be scary as hell.

First, it requires practice using a muscle that may have only been saved for a select few, if any. Second, the voices …

Oh my God, don't say that—they'll think you're crazy.

Well, you are crazy. But do you want people to know?

Okay, people may already know. But do you want them to know just HOW crazy you are? Nobody will know what you are talking about, they won't understand.

Nobody will get you.

Don't do this.

As I'm writing this, I'm actually choosing to distract myself, because it's really scary to be sharing the thoughts in my head out loud and even more so to have them published. So right now, I've made the beach my office as I write, so there will be fewer distractions. But somehow, I've decided it's extremely important to text my boyfriend thoughts and emojis about being naked at the beach ... and, I didn't leave my phone at home. It's fascinating watching the ego at work!

When Jane first asked me to be a part of this amazing collaboration, I could feel my cells and most of my entire being saying *yes*. And then ... there was my brain. I even said this to her, "I am not a writer. I mean, yes, I journal. But write and get published? I think you have the wrong gal."

She sweetly says, "Honey, I know this is for you. You are a storyteller."

I think to myself, hmmmm, a storyteller. Okay, maybe. But a writer? No way.

And, then she says, "And, this isn't a book talking about what you do in the world or what you've accomplished. I want you to write about whatever you don't want to write about. This needs to be raw and real. We're going to show the many different aspects of the Divine Feminine through many different women—REAL women."

Imagine the movie *Who Framed Roger Rabbit* (yes, I'm dating myself here), where Roger Rabbit's eyes are bulging a foot or two out of his eye sockets. Well, that was me. I feel like I've done such a great job keeping my craziness at least a little hidden ... I felt such an incredible "I know this is right for me AND, I really don't want to do this." I just wanted to run.

Alright, back to the uncomfortable place of the thoughts in my head and about sharing publicly.

People are going to think you're mean, stupid, a pushover, a wimp, a control freak, a freak, bossy, nagging, that you think waaaaayyyy too much.

They're going to see you for what you are—a fraud.

Why, oh why, do you want to do this?

You can never take this away.

You think you can start your business after people read this and are able to read all about you for the rest of time? Nobody will ever take you seriously after this.

And this brings me to the next part …

FEAR

There are many fears that come up, such as the fear of being too big. "You are too big for your britches," my mom used to say often as I was growing up. And, just to be clear in this moment, I *am* too big for my britches, literally. I'm totally chubby right now. Mostly, I'm okay with this, and then there's the voices …

You can't get up on a stage and talk to people at a yoga conference about how to make this world a better place looking the way you do—I mean, it's a yoga conference. Everyone there is skinny or at least in great shape. You're supposed to look a certain way. People won't trust you, believe you, won't want to stand with you and your vision, or take the actions it will take to fulfill that vision. People won't think that you can actually do anything to help them save the world if you aren't taking pristine care of your body.

And, you'll never believe what just happened in real time … Yup, distracting myself again.

Oh, I should take a picture of where I am writing this and post it to social media—writing essentials: a beach, my drum, a book, my water bottle with the Sri Yantra etched onto it. Because of course people want to know about my writing ways … Insert eye-rolling emoji. Okay, and a winking one, too.

But, I digress again. Back to the "too big for your britches" (ironically, I'm only 5 foot 3). Do you ever pay attention to all the thoughts? It's crazy-making, and yet most of us choose to sit and suffer and think that we are all alone and we are absolutely nuts. Or, we're not aware and those "behind the scene thoughts" are running our lives, or, as one of my coaches has said, "Who's driving your bus?" This kind of internal suffering is horrible, and it also makes it really easy for narcissists to come in and play their games with us. Just bringing awareness, because this is a whole other story.

What you are reading is a true test of my own vulnerability. Are you beginning to see how challenging it can be to be vulnerable?! Especially for a woman warrior spirit? I'd like to touch on this aspect for a second. We warrior women seem so tough, so courageous, so invincible—the first two may be true to an extent, but we're also super sensitive. We may even be more sensitive than most. One of the reasons we stand up for those who can't is that we can feel their pain. We also have very strong walls and masks; if we didn't, how could we fight as hard as we do for what we believe in? We'd always be sitting around crying!

Okay, back to my britches. I've always had a hard time fitting in. I was told I'm too loud. Too fierce, too tender, too daring, too sensitive, too crazy, too insensitive, too bossy, too, too, too … For a young girl, I just didn't fit into the quieter, pleasing version of how girls were "supposed" to be. I hung with the guys growing up. I didn't know how to be with my warrior (or my introvert, sensitive one, bosslady, or emotional self, either) as a woman. I didn't have a lot of role models of femininity. So, I was very masculine, at least I thought I was. Sometimes, I think I outdid some of the guys at being more like a dude. And, most of them didn't really look at me as girlfriend material—I was and am mostly heterosexual. I did have a tight group of guy friends with a few good girlfriends, though one of my best girlfriends couldn't handle who I was and ended our friendship. That was heartbreaking. I thought for sure I had found at least one girl who got me.

Where do I belong? I asked myself this often. *Who are my people?* Well, it was going to be a while before I found them … Not because they weren't around but because I chose to try to be different than who I was. This showed up as inauthenticity, at least on an energetic level, and we all know what that feels like to either be fake or be around someone who is—you don't really know how to navigate or converse or be real. And—*hello!*—I was giving away my power! So, I had this internal battle going on. I was trying to be more like the other girls, and my rebel (who was very strong inside of me) was like, *fuck this.* In other words, the true Me was nowhere to be found.

I actually became afraid of myself. Since I scared others away, I assumed I must be scary. I started consciously believing that I was bad, which had originated a lot earlier in my life and continues to be a limiting belief that shows up at times. I started believing that other people knew so much more than me—I mean, if they can figure out how to have awesome, healthy social interactions but I can't, obviously they knew more than me. They were better than me. Smarter than me. Prettier than me. You know how it goes … on and on and on …

GRIEF

Fast forward to present day. A week ago, while in the middle of this writing project, I was getting bodywork done from this amazing man, Reverend Jack Collins. I'd been seeing him for Trigger Point Release Therapy—ironically sort of like this writing project! A session with Jack is not just about physical healing but energy healing too. He was working on my neck and while he's "triggering" me I'm thinking "there's no way this neck pain can all be from this lifetime."

He then moved to a point above my ears, and I started feeling emotional. I wonder, "Is there a story or a memory with this?" *No* ... So, I decided to just let the emotions keep flowing without having to know why. A couple of minutes later, I was flooded with visions of past lives. Most of these visions were mine but some were others' (and gratefully I knew the difference). There were some visions of death-eater-like energies also—please understand that this isn't easy to share; it's that value of transparency of mine that's making me do it. It was all quite scary and uncomfortable, but I just kept allowing it to flow. I had some resistance come up here and there but just kept coming back to "I'm just going to be with this."

After he finished working on me, he asked me if I'd like to talk about what came up. I'm not sure what had just happened ... So, I told him all of that. I was still bawling. I knew that the grieving floodgates were open, and I was willing to be with it. He asked me if I heard a sound, that sometimes these things will have a sound to them. First, I can't believe he asks me this ... Second, I'm so ashamed to tell him, but I did. You know, that transparency thing. I tell him that there was a scream.

You have to understand, this is a composed, calm man, but I could feel his excitement, even though he was containing it.

His words to me were so soothing and beautiful and yet didn't bring me out of my grief. He says, "The scream is actually you screaming for you to connect with *yourself*. Picture it like this: You are screaming. There is this layer of earthen material (which may appear like shit). And then, there is the *you* that you are right here. The shit layer is all of those scary memories and visions, but you have to dig into that shit to get to You. And, the grief that you are feeling is not grief for what happened in all of those lifetimes. It is the grief of You knowing that the outcome could be different, and yet it isn't. There is also a knowing of having a deep spiritual purpose that you are still longing to fulfill—both in those lives that ended looking like "failures" and this one that we're living. We are, after all, here in this human experience looking for understanding."

I left there that day, still bawling and contemplating my grief. I got really good at grieving a couple of years ago while going through my divorce. I got so good, that I would say I was happy to be grieving. I know, that may sound strange. I chose to grieve that relationship fully—for my health, for the health of my future relationships, for my children. I wanted to show my children that you can grieve while still being happy at times. Grieving doesn't mean going into a full depression for months. It is simply giving yourself the space to be with whatever comes up, no matter what. And, maybe just maybe, I gave other people in the community "permission" to do the same. We are not typically a grieving culture, so it is powerful!

Throughout my divorce, I would go running at a public bird sanctuary where people go to walk, run, watch birds, and watch the sunset. Often, I'd listen to musician John Trudell and would be bawling as I ran. And, sometimes, I would end up doubled over screaming and swearing! Yup, that was me. I'm sure there may have been some parents telling their children to not talk to me or turning right around. But this was a big turning point for me to take my power back.

After that tremendous experience with my body worker/reverend, it's been very interesting to witness my inner world. That first week after, I wanted so badly to just be with my Self. I wanted to dig into the shit and reconnect with that part of me—the part that is screaming for *me*. I just wanted to feel whole. I'm sure many can relate, for those of us who are on this journey of personal growth, we want to finally feel like we've gotten somewhere … that the searching is done … that we figured it out, and we can just coast from here. Well, I'm not sure that ever happens. That first week, of course, all these things came up. My boyfriend's dog ended up having to get surgery. *A little side-note: I live pretty far from a big city, so we have to drive almost four hours to get him to a vet who can do this. I love his dog. I love him. So, of course the ever-giving part of me tells him I will go with him. Another little side note: I'm a super busy, crazy entrepreneur who has a million things going on.* So, not only am I taking myself away from the many hours of work that need to get done, I'm also not giving my Self the time that She wants and needs. Oh, how the ego wants to protect itself and not allow us to see it and yet runs the show anyway! All of these other things definitely need my attention, right?

We are taught to give our power away as we grow up. It's inevitable. It could be from us saying what we want to our parents, and them yelling at us for it. (There is no blame in this statement—I am a firm believer that we are all doing the best that we can. And, those of us who've been through harder situations have a choice; we can either keep the generational wounds going or we can find new ways.) It can be from things that are said to us, such as "Being too big for our britches." Again, I'm not blaming or feeling sorry for myself. I love my mom dearly, and she was just looking out for me. And, if that wouldn't have happened, I might not be here right now to share my story with you from the place that I am. And, honestly, being too big for my britches since the day I was born also gives me power now—knowing that I am a powerhouse!

Giving away our power is as much about not being aware of the thoughts in our head and letting them run our lives as it is thinking that other people can do it better than us. Or, by not giving our Self the time and space that she needs to reconnect. Power loss can also come from fear. Trying to be someone we're not can leave us feeling really lost, confused, scared, and desperate

So, how do we get our power back?

Well, this can be easy and also challenging at the same time—it's definitely a paradox. And, there's a lot to be said about accepting the paradoxes in life.

The following are some of the things that I've done. I share them with you to give you some ideas. If they resonate, give them a try!

First, **get quiet, connect with your soul, and see what is in alignment with you.** Since we are all different and process things differently, we must always do that.

Listen to what the voices in your head are saying, preferably without judgment. It has really amazed me to be told by some people that they don't have any inner dialogue going on. That one really made me feel crazy for a while. Since then, I've come to find that we all have these internal conversations. So, listen to the voices—some are insightful, some are just trying to cause problems, some are trying to talk you out of things. Most importantly, understand that those voices aren't you.

Accept and acknowledge who you are. Some of the things we learn about ourselves we may not be comfortable with, but accept them anyways. For instance, this strong, warrior woman likes validation as a form of love. I don't love this fact, but it is what it is, and it's a lot easier to know it and share it.

Use your voice and share your truth. Your voice is such a power center. There's a beautiful synergy that happens when the mind and heart are connected. The throat is in the middle of that. So, as long as you are operating out of both mind *and* heart, the throat gets to go along for a beautiful ride, when you open her up!

Always, always, always ask yourself, "What do I want?" I've watched it over and over. The first time I was asked this by someone, or the times I've asked other people, we tend to get teary-eyed. It's a really big deal when someone cares enough to ask what you want.

And, of course, **be gentle with yourself, forgive yourself, and know that this is a practice.** Nobody starts out as an expert at anything. As Brené Brown says, *Talk to yourself like you would to a child.*

I don't have this all figured out. And, honestly I don't know if I ever will. We are all energy, and energy is always changing forms and shapes—so will the layers of what we are to be working on. And, I could be totally wrong, too! But it's a journey that I will keep walking, because in all of its seasons, life is an amazing adventure. I know that my Soul is here to do something in service to humanity.

I also know that when I am in my power, it will be actualized in this lifetime.

Cristina Laskar is the founder of Connectavid, a website for connection, collaboration, and contribution to build strong communities around causes. Connectavid is a place for users to confidently share their voice, to strengthen connections, and to impart knowledge. It's the meeting ground for leaders to find help, understanding, and to embrace limitless possibilities. As a facilitator for fully integrated healing, Cristina Laskar was formerly a Wholistic Healthcare Practitioner. She started Connectavid as a way to ask us to remember our true nature and to live accordingly. Her background in Ayurveda and Traditional Chinese Medicine, and certification in Ayurvedic massage and Marma therapy helped chart this path. Cristina's passion for healing led her to create Connectavid in order to have a larger impact that brings lasting change. Connectavid's mission is to inspire awareness, acceptance, and responsibility—to bring about progressive leadership towards an empowered future. Connectavid is passionate about keeping it light, but sincere. Its goal is to find ways to play, interact, and to do something unusual. It's a place to cultivate good listening, with a nod to bettering this planet and its inhabitants for countless generations. The heart of Connectavid lies in reminding people that we're all in this together and to empower people to take charge. As we find our health, happiness, and limitless love within, we become more aware that we can only make change together. Cristina is a mother of two teenage boys who inspired her to learn about health and healing. They also gave her a great desire to leave this planet in a better place for them and future generations. Contact Cristina via direct message at **www.connectavid.com.** And, if you create your free profile, they'll plant a tree for you with Eden Reforestation Projects!

Freeing the Goddess

BY NAIA LEIGH

A new species of woman is emerging and is evolving into something this world has never seen.

The Goddess is rising ... and being remembered in the hearts and souls of humanity once again. She is the essence of what makes us women. She is the heart that holds the world, and the beauty that paints it. She is the bountiful and boundless force that has gone unrecognized, undervalued, suppressed, abused, and even killed in many of our cultures for thousands of years. And *we*, my sister, are here to change that.

As I did, most women longed for something, yet may not have known what it was. We may have filled this void with attachments such as food, shopping, wine, or the wrong relationships. We may have worked too hard, played too much, or made sure everyone else was happy, while we ignored that subtle ache inside. Even though our desires may have led us to think that this missing piece resided in our partner's love, our boss's approval, more money, a perfect body, or finishing our to-do list, what we crave deep down is in none of those.

What women's souls have been really crying out for ... is *ourselves*.

It is the taste, the touch, and the feeling of our own essence. We yearn for the feminine face of God that runs through our veins that wasn't taught to us in school or church. It is the communion with our *boundless* Nature that we long to know.

Deep down, we yearn to reunite with the raw, wild, feminine, and untamed side of ourselves. It is the passionate feeler, inspired creator, and sensual goddess that we miss. It is the healer and the shaman we've been afraid to admit exists. It is our emotions and our inner warrioress and empowers and liberates us. It is the ancient, wise, and all-knowing Earth Mother that always has the answer. It is our rebel, leader, and risk taker that will make the impact we wish to create. And it is our unabashed lover who seeks to serve and to heal the world back into wholeness. These are the parts that we were told didn't exist. These are the parts that didn't feel safe in the world.

Through all the Earth's phases of time and space and all the identities we've had as women, one thing has remained the same: Women have gotten to know who "woman" is through a tainted, patriarchal lens. We have lived in a world designed and defined by men, a world that largely devalues, discourages, and dishonors the gifts and needs of the feminine spirit.

As we absorbed the masculinized teachings of the patriarchal game, we adapted to it ensure our success and survival.

At times, we had to silence our feminine voices, gifts, needs, emotions, desires, talents, and intuitions. We went to "his" schools, accepted his account of his-story, obeyed his political leadership, worked his jobs, wore his clothes, spoke his language, had his sex, and saw his doctors. We forgot our magical abilities and boundless power, because it wasn't welcome at the patriarchal table. All along, Woman has measured her worth with a faulty measuring stick, one that more accurately resembles a double-edged sword, etched with an imbalanced scale of measurement. Most women have, as I did, adopted this sword as their own personal measure of self-worth, endlessly reminding ourselves of where we fall short, and unconsciously using it to sever the pieces of ourselves that didn't fit in.

Most women are born open, free, and connected to their feminine Nature. Our inner Goddess was alive and trusting of life. We were once unapologetically creative, imaginative, emotional, and sensual. We were tapped into the beauty, and the pain, of the world. We cried when we were sad and threw tantrums when we were mad. We said what we meant, sang when we felt like it, and danced our hearts out, no matter who was looking. We didn't give a crap about how we looked, we loved strangers, and we played in the mud. And then, as time went on, we learned to ignore the impulses of our feminine inspirations; we learned to obey. We learned to value the teachings of the authority figures in our lives who wanted to teach us how to succeed in this world. The only problem was that we were not meant to contribute to the world we were born into, we came to create a new one.

I, like many women, wasn't taught about the beauty, power, and honor of being a woman. I wasn't taught about the Goddess, the intelligence of my own body, the magic of my cycle, or my creative purpose. I wasn't taught about my ancient wisdom, or the sacred value in sisterhood, or how our sensuality is a gateway to our divinity and feminine power.

I was told that Eve came from Adam's rib and was exiled for exercising her birthright and taste the fruits of the Earth, and she was shamed for her nakedness. I was taught about women's value through music videos, commercials, and ads that commoditize women's sexuality. I learned to think of my monthly cycle as a burden and to hide it. I learned in school and at home that girls judge, get jealous, and betray one another. I was told to pick a career, go to college, and work for a boss the rest of my life. I saw that older white men with a lot of money make the rules and get their way, no matter whose well-being it compromises. I saw that we are destroying the planet for corporate profit. None of this felt right, but it was normal, just like poverty, rape, and war.

Even though something felt wrong, I couldn't put my finger on what, exactly. I was unaware of the patriarchal waters that I swam in, and unaware that there was even another way.

I took a women's studies class in college, and I sat in the back of the room, rolling my eyes as I listened to the teachers going on and on about the injustices women have faced. I heard about unequal pay and objectification in the media, but I couldn't help but feel … "What's the big deal?" Women could vote and get any job we wanted, and they were willing participants in being sexy in the media. I knew nothing else.

It wasn't until I was physically, emotionally, and spiritually brought to my knees, that I found out who my inner Goddess was and what she had to say about it all.

RESURRECTING MY GODDESS

I grew up in a Midwest Catholic family, the daughter of an eighteen-year-old college student. My mother loved me, although she did not know how to show me the way I needed. As the years passed, she became more cold, critical, and strict. Even when I was young, I understood that my happiness, good fortune, or brightness would trigger her and create undesirable consequences for me. Because of this, I learned to hide and think quite lowly of myself. I found myself desperately longing for a what felt like a "normal" mother-daughter relationship. I wanted to laugh, cuddle, learn feminine wisdom, and go shopping and talk about boys. For most of my life, I carried deep anxiety that I felt at home and around other women, assuming they would judge, sabotage, and disapprove of me.

This carried into my school life as most of my female friendships ended in some betrayal or misunderstanding. In high school, as most coming-of-age-women experience, I started receiving more attention for my appearance and quickly observed that this was how I could be seen and get the love that I so desperately craved. I started dressing more feminine, and although I received attention from men I found that women became even more cruel. The summer of my junior year, my breasts developed quickly. When I returned to school my entire class was convinced I had gotten breast implants, and I was given the nickname of a popular porn star. I started hearing a new false rumor about myself almost daily and often heard the word "slut" uttered as I walked through the halls. Cruel words were written about me on my locker and in bathroom stalls, and I had bottles thrown at my head. During lunch one day, I was humiliated when the football team called me over at lunch to ask if I had slept with the entire team, in front of all of everyone (even though I hadn't been with a single one of them). I began to sit by myself between the lockers for lunch. I felt unseen and misunderstood at home and at school and learned more and more to live life in a state of apology for being me.

Much of what I knew about being a woman were feelings of disconnection, shame, competition, and objectification. My sensuality and the love that I had for people was misunderstood and misguided. Eventually I just became what they projected on to me: a flirtatious and promiscuous lush. At least this way I could escape and have some fun. Boys, alcohol, and dissociation distracted me from the feelings I was trying to avoid. It wasn't until my early twenties that it became clear that something needed to change. In college I began to further pursue my interests in art, spirituality, and healing. And the more I pursued these things, the less I craved my old life and the less I could mask my pain with alcohol and promiscuity.

To rise like the phoenix, I needed to go
through the fire.

During this time, it became clear that I didn't have many memories. I knew most things that had happened, although I had blocked out most of my life, sparing some photographic instances. As it turns out, I had amnesia. When I stopped drinking, I had to confront my underlying issues, including anxiety, chronic insomnia, increasing physical illness, grief, deep longing, and emptiness.

I desperately sought answers and healing for these things, reading as many metaphysical and self-help books as I could get my hands on and traveling for healing workshops. I found my spiritual home in a Therapeutic Life Coaching program that taught subconscious reprogramming, hypnosis, and metaphysics. I finally found like-minded people who could see me for who I was (as much as I could show at that time). This was a safe place where I could explore why I felt so broken.

Through this exploration I uncovered something that would change my life forever. Psychics, healers, and shamans had all alluded to a violation of boundaries in my past, and I ignored it until it revealed itself directly to me. My father partied with friends and struggled with alcoholism and cocaine addiction. He would invite friends over from time to time, one of whom would visit my bedroom at night when I was five. I finally saw how my adult symptoms of feeling violated, alone, and unprotected related to this experience as a child. It explained everything. No wonder I had amnesia. No wonder I was always anxious and couldn't sleep for weeks at a time. This explained why I never really trusted men or let myself fall in love. I understood why I was always sick to my stomach and would break down sobbing without knowing why. I now knew why I had never felt truly safe.

I shared my story—and discovered that just about every woman I knew also had a story of violation.

Uncovering this avalanche of trauma took its toll; and my health began to deteriorate and my outward appearance began to reflect the wounding of my internal world. I lost much of my hair, gained weight, looked pregnant, and had large bags under my eyes. More than ever, I couldn't be seen for who I was.

The time had come to stop being defined by my past and take my power back. I confronted my parents and took space from them, allowing myself to find who I was outside of the painful dynamics of my family. Because my relationship interactions with men came from a wounded place, I chose to be celibate for a couple of years. I ended friendships that couldn't meet my evolving values and interests. I let myself feel my deepest despair, longing, grief, and anger. I ate healthier. I read and spent more time in nature. I moved to the West Coast to find my soul family. I cried myself to sleep many nights. I forgave my abuser. I healed my relationship with my mother and connected with the feminine face of the Divine. I began channeling this essence through art and sacred dance. I began to love my womb, cycle, and yoni (vagina) in a way I never thought possible. I learned to trust my intuition and soulful inspiration above anything else outside me. I learned to trust and open to women in my life. I sat with sisters in ceremony, holding one another through the deepest of our shadows and supporting one another's greatest dreams. I co-developed a healing modality I now call Boundless* that helped me heal the many layers that were weighing me down. I experienced a Kundalini awakening and, still today, experience waves of pleasure and healing throughout my body. I and began to open and trust men for the first time, and I met my current partner who loves honors me very deeply.

I had never known that such satisfaction in womanhood even existed. I finally felt that I had a purpose, and this was to remind every woman about the boundless beauty and power that lies within her. I started writing about and painting depictions of this boundless feminine power and began working exclusively with women to heal their blocks to unleashing their creative voice in the world. I started writing articles and leading women's circles, helping women to liberate this place of pleasure and empowerment within themselves. Today I do my best to give women the love and insights that I didn't have growing up.

I found that reclaiming our feminine wisdom, power, and voice asks us to have the courage to dig deep into the depths of our darkest inner soil to plant new seeds of our brightest future. We are being asked now to *feel*. To love our shadows back into the light. To feel what it was like to lose her and to give her the space to express and release what she couldn't then.

GODDESSES PAINT A NEW WORLD

We've all had reasons to play small, hide, or to protect our inner Goddess. But right now is a rare and special time in history. Now is the time that the stars and the prophecies speak of. It is now, and only now, that we have the collective freedom and resources to make monumental change. Today's Goddess calls on ancient wisdom and also makes use of modern technologies. Anything is possible now. And when we come together we become an unstoppable feminine force.

This soulful feminine movement is not led by a guru, an activist or a politician. This is a mass awakening and collective co-creation. This is us, walking one another home, one step at a time. Each time we give our love, speak our truth, heal our individual and collective wounds, give our gifts, and uplift one another, we pave the way to freeing the Goddess everywhere.

We are not meant to hide the very essence that is the antidote to the madness in the world. We were made to embody our inner Goddess so brightly that we ignite each other's remembrance. When we free our Goddess from her prison, we create a world that fosters and protects the Goddess within every woman. If each woman knew her Goddess and listened to and expressed her feminine voice, the world would be a far more beautiful, peaceful, and thriving place. If each woman were to step into her feminine wisdom, power, and gifts, I truly believe that our global issues would be solved.

By no means am I saying that we are all meant to be in the public eye as political leaders, authors, speakers, or activists. Quite the opposite. The love and voice of the feminine is needed in every corner of the universe, in every family, community, school, park, and hospital. Our love, passion and purpose is needed in our media, political, medical, social, religious, and judicial systems. We are being called to walk as leaders, healers, teachers, and mentors. We are meant to be the wise women that we didn't have and to model the best qualities in the ones we did. And in doing so we are reminded that we are a part of an ancient sisterhood that supports one another to shine brighter than ever—together.

If you know your inner Goddess, it is my deepest wish that you are protecting her with everything you've got … claiming her more deeply every day, in every interaction, and fighting for her life as if it carries the antidote to the world's psychosis … because she does.

If you have not yet tasted the power and pleasure of Her, it is my even deeper wish that you will lovingly yet fiercely create the space for Her to come alive again. To discover who she is, what inspires her, and how she longs to express herself through you. To dive into the depths of her caves and retrieve your innermost treasure. The Goddess lives on, but needs us—her daughters—to bring her back stronger than ever.

The greatest hoax in human history was convincing women that we have no power and that pleasure is a sin. *In truth, we carry the power of the Earth within our wombs, and our pleasure is the cosmic act of divine creation.* It may have taken exile, witch hunts, the demoralization of Mary Magdalene, media objectification, violation, and religious shaming to convince Her otherwise. But only for a few thousand years. His-story has reached its long-awaited end and Her-story is being written as we speak. Our fires may have been put out for a time, but Her embers remained, glowing brightly in carefully chosen places … awaiting *this* moment.

By embodying our feminine nature today, we become leaders of a new era in which we no longer mold ourselves to fit into the world but instead mold the world to fit us. Through the inspiration of soul, the love for one another, and the courage to carve new paths, we create a better world for future generations.

It's time.

Thank you for sharing the journey.

Naia Leigh thrives on life's beauty, creativity and supporting others in discovering their passion and purpose. She is an international women's empowerment coach, writer, and artist and guides both the individual and collective process of women's empowerment. She is the co-founder of Boundless®, a modality that clears the root causes of blockages, and she leads international retreats and Boundless trainings. Confronted at an early age with many emotional and physical healing challenges, Naia has been on a long, powerful journey to overcome and heal anxiety, sexual abuse, illness and other mental, physical, and emotional challenges. By the age of twenty-one, she completed her Therapeutic Life Coaching certification and studied modalities such as neuro-linguistic programming (NLP), Past Life Regression therapy, breathwork and channeling. In 2012 Naia was guided to live on Kauai to go deeper into her healing process and to co-develop a cutting-edge modality she named "Boundless"—a core-healing method that efficiently uncovers and clears the root causes of issues and blockages preventing forward growth. Boundless enabled Naia to actively step more fully into her life purpose and creative gifts, and be of greater service to women and the planet. She empowers women through supporting the emergence of greater sensuality, purpose, creativity, and personal power. Her mission is to create sacred space for women to reunite, heal, and empower one another to be all that they are and support a new feminine leadership in the world. Learn more: ***www.NaiaLeigh.com***

Jewels in the Darkness:
Unearthing My Feminine Rhythm

BY TANYA LYNN

"Do you *want* to become a mother?"

The words stopped time. Alone with my soul, I felt silence dripping like wet paint all over me, covering me like a veil. Enshrouded in the most important question of my life, I closed my eyes and sat without moving, listening for something, my soul to speak, my soul to nudge me, my soul to guide me to the answer.

For the four months prior to Karen asking me this question, I had written it off. I didn't really feel the call; motherhood did not feel like it was the path for me. I knew what I wanted and that was to make a difference on this planet, and I was afraid that motherhood would put a big damper on that dream, taking me out of my power and into a form of slavery. If I chose motherhood, I would be confined to making a difference for that one child (or two). Not the world. I couldn't see an "and" in the equation, only an "either/or."

But in that moment of silence, a feeling arose from deep within my core, from the seat of my womb, and it bubbled up into my heart and came out of my mouth as a barely audible "Yes."

Yes. Even despite the fear of giving up my dreams to be like my own mother whose sole purpose was to be a mother.

Yes. I said it louder, witnessed by my friend Karen.

And as if that "yes" was a pebble dropped into the ocean, the ripples began to expand outward in that moment, creating a tsunami that would drastically transform the course of my life faster than I could ever imagine.

Our words carry tremendous power.

In physics, power is the output of energy dependent on the weight (or mass of the object) and its velocity.

When we speak something into existence, and we say it in a way that carries a lot of weight through a declaration that has emphasis and meaning, its energy can be massive like a tidal wave. Those words can create new circumstances that support that declaration, new opportunities to help it be manifested.

In my case, an opportunity came into my life to heal and release all the fear that arose with that declaration. And when I say heal, I really mean that I completely fell apart, unraveled and fell into an abyss of darkness for six months in what I call "My Dark Night of the Soul."

We have become so entangled in the limited belief that "a mother can only be a mother and on top of that, she must be a self-sacrificing mother." The Martyr Mother is praised by our culture so that any woman who questions her desire of becoming a mother is ridiculed and shamed for going against the system. And any mother who puts herself first is also shamed and ridiculed for being selfish, a disruption of the status quo.

I knew there was another way. Another archetype who embodied both the healthy mother and the healthy queen. A woman who could both nurture her young *and* lead in the world *without* burning herself out. A woman who could meet her own needs, the needs of her family, and the needs of her community.

To get there, a woman must first unravel the conditioning that has been passed down to her from generation to generation. She must let go of the temptation to be the martyr mother and all the glory she would receive from society for being such an obedient, good, perfect supermom.

She must get messy and allow herself to let go of the facade of perfection, having it all together, and doing it all by herself.

She must call in sisterhood and allow herself to get vulnerable about her fears, challenges, and emotions in a circle of other women who can then hold her, love her, and support her.

She must understand the nature of her feminine essence and sync up with the cycles and rhythms of her body to find a flow that nourishes rather than drains her.

For me, this meant letting go of everything I thought I was and everything I thought I wanted to be. Essentially, I needed to kill off all the identities and roles I played, past, present and future, and discover the truth of who I was underneath it all.

My Dark Night of the Soul was a period of immense suffering as I let go of goals, dreams, aspirations, and beliefs about who I was and who I would be. I let go of my business. It felt like I was in a cocoon, or a womb, trapped with nowhere to go, nowhere to hide, completely enveloped in darkness. Unable to see the way out. Complete surrender and trust in the process of being reborn out of nothingness.

Sounds terrible ... and it was. I thrashed and cried and kicked and screamed.

But despite the misery of those eight months, I learned to trust the dark mysterious ways of the feminine and to know myself as the purest essence of woman in body, mind, and spirit. I understood, and was in awe of, the miracle of being born a woman in this lifetime with the ability to birth both babies *and* a soul aligned global business. I realized that the two were inseparable, linked, and intertwined.

My purpose was not to save the world but to be the living, breathing example of a conscious woman embodied in her power.

Nine months after that declaration, I met Brent, the man who would be the father of my future daughters. And I published my first book, which would become the foundation of my business.

Exactly one year after that declaration, I found out I was pregnant.

Life started to move at warp speed as soon as I emerged from the darkness. For the first time in my life, I felt alive. Really alive. Present. Able to feel all of my feelings in all of their intensity without fear of them overwhelming me. The more intensely I felt my sadness and rage, the more access I had to feeling joy and love. It felt exhilarating, freeing, and magnificent.

Brent and I traveled and played and worked together. We were all in. He supported me as I grew my business from a place of grounded power and unwavering faith without getting sucked into the rat race of needing to prove myself capable, worthy, or popular.

When Kali was born, the flow felt natural and effortless. Because of my intentions, the clearing work I did during my Dark Night of the Soul, and the commitment I had to being the example of feminine leadership, Kali fell right in sync with our lives. Brent and I both focused on making sure our individual cups were full and, as a result, Kali was getting all of her needs met from our overflow. We found a rhythm that helped our baby sleep well and fuss little.

While I watched so many other moms around me struggling with a lack of sleep, self-care, and quality time alone with their partners, I was fully aware that I had created something evolutionary, a new model for women to step into being a mother without compromising themselves, their relationship, their baby, or their business.

This is not to say that everything was smooth sailing with clear sunny skies for long.

I wanted to embody the Mother Queen archetype, balancing the healthy qualities of two powerful divine feminine archetypes: The Mother being a woman who exudes unconditional love, compassion, and acceptance and takes care of herself and those around her (including the earth), and the Queen being a woman who stands powerfully in her conviction, living out her purpose to serve the world from her the heart in a sustainable way. But, if I was to walk this path and set a new precedent for feminine leadership, I had to pass through many initiation gates. I had to face some intense challenges to test my unwavering faith and courage.

I had to integrate the unstoppable Warrioress, my own internal Kali who would slash through any and all illusions that the old patriarchal paradigm tried to throw at me to take me out of my power. I bought into the lie that only when I had achieved success (by creating a huge global movement), would I be worthy of living. My whole existence was based on working hard and sacrificing myself to "change the world." I was constantly pushing, striving, and giving from my masculine strengths, burning myself out because I ignored the natural rhythm of my body and never opened myself up to receive or rest. I lived my life as one big *exhale*.

The truth is, life is cyclical as seen in nature all around us: the dark of night and the light of day, the rise and fall of the tide, the ever-changing seasons.

Life is constantly expanding and contracting, one big *inhale* followed by an *exhale* repeated over and over again.

Understanding the law of impermanence is key to our liberation. Our power, as women, is directly related to how well we navigate the ups and downs and allow ourselves to surrender to our natural cycles of light and dark.

If I surrendered to the dark, if I truly detached from my identity as the "global change agent," who would I be? Would I matter? Would anyone still love me? Would I be forgotten, isolated, left out, or even ostracized?

It's only when we stop judging the dark that
we will be free.

Going through My Dark Night of the Soul prepared me to face two of the most difficult challenges during my second year of motherhood. It gave me the awareness and the tools to navigate the choppy waters of the storm coming my way: the loss of my baby and the loss of my business as I knew it.

Unfortunately, I left my most important tool on shore when I set off for sea: my intuition.

During our honeymoon nine months after Kali was born, despite the nagging little voice that told me we shouldn't, we tried again … and got pregnant again. Something felt off. The idea of having two under two didn't feel right. It felt forced, like we were rushing it to get it over with, not the best intention to bring a soul into this world.

Professionally, I had a launch lined up and felt an enormous amount of pressure to keep the momentum rolling.

The day after my launch, I miscarried. For three days, my body released copious amounts of blood, clots, and tissue. For three days, I released tears of fear, grief, guilt, and remorse.

I was devastated. But instead of honoring my body physically and emotionally, I dove right back into my work and got into a business partnership with one of my best friends … despite that little nagging voice that said, "Don't do business with friends unless you want to ruin it like you did last time."

Again, I ignored my intuition, as if I didn't understand her language quite yet.

I got caught in the old pattern of forcing work to avoid the darkness, but it inevitably caught up with me.

If only I would have given myself space after that miscarriage to sit in the pain and mourning.

If only I would have honored the cycle of death that was happening to allow myself to heal and become reborn again.

If only I would have …

The judgment of the darkness made it worse. But the judgment led me to an even bigger period of struggle, a more powerful initiation into my evolutionary leadership … so there is no point in judging my judgment.

After four months of working together, my friend and I split.

I spun out. I crashed. I burned.

It rocked both of our worlds. Hurt, jealousy, competition, betrayal. We both walked away with our tails between our legs, unable to come back together in friendship for another year.

This time, I surrendered to the darkness and let it envelop me once again. Whenever I would fight it, I lost. So I stayed there.

We've been conditioned to keep running, to stay positive, to keep our heads up and our hearts protected. When we put our life on high gear, we keep our emotions at check so they don't derail us. The faster we go, the harder it is to slow down.

Until we crash and burn.

The numbers are staggering for women with adrenal fatigue, thyroid conditions, and a general sense of burnout. It's because we judge the dark, we judge the emotions that lie buried in the dark, and we judge ourselves for having those feelings.

But the continual movement upward, trying to keep the peak going as long as possible, trying to stay happy, inspired, and on point all the time is exhausting. It's nauseating. It's making us sick. It's keeping us tied up and enslaved to the old patriarchal paradigm.

As I surrendered this time to the darkness and allowed myself to go into the void of the unknown mystery, I could actually hear and tune into the song of my soul again. I could see where I had misstepped and get back in alignment, back in harmony.

And as I felt around in that dark cave, I stumbled upon some very valuable jewels. I unearthed some precious gems.

A diamond that showed me that I'm worthy of love without doing anything.

A ruby that showed me when to push and when to relax.

A sapphire that showed me how to receive the support and contribution surrounding me.

An emerald that showed me how to take care of myself so I can give from overflow so I don't burn out.

An amethyst that showed me how to identify, ask for, and receive what I need.

> The jewels are buried deep within Mother
> Earth. We have to dig around in the dark to
> find them.

You, my dear sister, may have so much fear around descending deep into the darkness, surrendering to the dark feminine, the Great Mother in all her mystery. She's dark. She's deep. She's muddy. She's vast. And in all of that enshrouded mysterious darkness, she is the activating source of all that is.

This is your source of power. This is your access to create. This is the activation of life energy on the planet.

Within the darkness. In the murky waters. In the depths of your own body, your own womb.

Before you can create, you must take a pregnant pause in the void. There is a reason pregnancy lasts nine months. That incubation time is crucial for the development of a child. Likewise, *your* development as a woman happens in the darkness, the pregnant pause, the void. We must honor it. We must revere it. We must allow it.

During that time after my friend and I split and I surrendered to the darkness, I healed, transformed, and realigned.

I got pregnant again, and this time, it felt divine.

I shifted my business again, and this time, it felt integrated.

Instead of pushing during the first trimester for this pregnancy, I rested. I listened to my body and the natural rhythm of the winter season.

As I entered week thirteen, I knew that I had three months to tap into the creative flow of second trimester and push my business forward into its next phase of growth. I went into focus-mode and produced some incredible results. Then, knowing my energy was going to tank, I slowed down and began my descent toward the birth, giving myself ample recovery and integration time.

This time, as I *chose* to go into darkness, knowing it was part of the cycle, I had my eyes wide open for insights and revelations. I searched for jewels in this cave that would serve me in the delivery of my next baby. All the while, I gathered a support team around me to keep the business and my household running so that I could relax and surrender into the natural rhythm of my body.

No longer judging, I trusted.

This is the path of the evolutionary woman. We are on the precipice of a new generation of feminine leaders who embody the Mother Queen, nurturing themselves, their children, their families, *and* their communities.

When we honor our body's natural energetic rhythm, we create magic. We find flow. We reclaim our worthiness as women without needing to prove ourselves capable of fitting in the old system.

Whether that is syncing up with your monthly menstrual cycle of ovulation and bleeding, the trimesters of pregnancy, or even the monthly moon cycles of menopause, you have to find your own intuitive and energetic rhythm to live your life in your own version of feminine flow and harmony.

This path is actually a *returning* to our natural state, a returning to the Great Mother in all her infinite wisdom. It is there we begin to embody unconditional love and acceptance of ourselves and one another.

It is from this place that we will change the world.

Tanya Lynn is a strategic activator, gifted at coaching women to soar to new heights by putting together a plan that maximizes their talents and strengths and taking bold, courageous actions to fulfill on their intentions. Tanya is the visionary CEO behind the international organization Sistership Circle, a worldwide sisterhood movement empowering women to step into their true beauty, brilliance, and boldness as feminine leaders. She started training facilitators to use her proven 12-week Circle Program based on her bestselling book "Open Your Heart: How to Be a New Generation Feminine Leader." She is also the author of "How to Lead Circle." She is a respected leader in the industry from clients and colleagues alike because she's the real deal, living and breathing her work. She believes that the new model of feminine leadership is not about hierarchies of power but about circles of collaboration. For us to become true leaders, we must embrace our sisters as our allies and give one another permission to shine. Learn more: www.sistershipcircle.com

Reclaiming Our Cycles

BY DR. MARIE MBOUNI

I made a promise to myself
to the universe
that I am committed to reclaiming my whole self
to be myself completely
to stand for who I am.
I made a promise that from now on
I will only show up in full color
authentic
Unapologetic
fully female
fully woman.
I made a promise to myself that I will do everything it takes
to get to the place where I finally feel whole
to the place where I am fully alive.

After Donald Trump became president of the United States, even as he was being accused by everyone of oppressing, suppressing, and belittling women, of not respecting them, and taking away their rights, I decided that I had to look at myself first. If Trump was in my reality, then I had to take radical responsibility for my own actions. I had to and stop and ask myself, "How am I doing to myself what he is accused of doing to women?"

I had to face the reality I had created for myself.

I started thinking, wait a minute, wait a minute, wait a minute! What does it mean to be a woman? An empowered woman? A successful woman? What kind of woman was I being? What kind of woman did I want to be? How was I showing up? Who was I being? With myself? With others?

I began this inquiry a few weeks after the election results.

The first shift that happened for me was to shift into love and to self-love, because when you love yourself enough, you don't need to suppress, oppress, shut down, or bully anybody else. Diving deep into self-love also helped me dive deep into my inner world.

I slowly came to the realization that, little by little, I had completely erased my femininity. Little by little, I had let my "woman" self disappear. Little by little, I had shut down anything that had to do with what it means to be feminine. I had cut out and shut down the parts of me that were open to receiving, vulnerable, and soft. I did things like a man because we've been taught to do it that way. We've been taught to embody more masculine than feminine energy in order to be successful, accepted, powerful, self-sufficient, and in control—not needing support or help from anyone.

This led me to the realization that I had, in essence, given myself a *spiritual and energetic hysterectomy*. I had abandoned the fundamental way women create and manifest, instead allowing societal pressures to control me. I was *full on* in the matrix. As I began observing women around me, I realized that so many awakened entrepreneurial and powerful women do the same thing!

Sisters, we don't have to be like men to be successful, accepted, powerful, self-sufficient, and in control. We were created to be women. The time is *now* for women to reclaim their cycles. The time is now for women to reclaim their full magnetic and creative powers! Now is the time to heal ourselves and our planet.

After this big realization, I made a promise to myself to make this my reality. Because now I am finally ready and committed to be myself. I have no other choice! I finally have the courage to show up and practice owning my femininity and my power.

What I'm suggesting is for women to be in ecstatic expression. We need the freedom to be who we are, to be sovereign, to be radically empowered by unleashing our sexual powers.

As Jane Ashley, the publisher of this book, says, "Together, collectively, we can create a resonating vibration of love and light to support and heal the world."

More than ever, in that moment of epiphany I became fully committed to heal my feminine and dive deep within to find answers.

I began meditating in nature.

Each morning, I went to the ocean to sit, hold my womb, and ask for guidance on how to become an empowered woman of the new paradigm. I asked the Great Mother Ocean to guide and support me. I realized that I had not even touched myself, or been present with my body in a very long time—because I was very busy *doing* rather than *being*.

I asked myself, "How did I become this unempowered woman—so different from how I imagined myself to be as an empowered woman who was fully present in her body and in touch with her sacred mysterious powers?"

Am I aware of my own power?
What does my fullest potential look like?
How am I using my power for good—or how am I abusing it?
Am I nurturing my connection to my higher source of energy?
What action can I take to move into a better direction?
What resources are available to me, and am I allowing the universe to help by tapping into them?

A sacred connection was being established with mama ocean.

REDEFINING WHAT IT MEANS TO BE A WOMAN

What does it mean to be a woman in this new paradigm?

> "Many Non-Western traditions state that the feminine is about receiving. However most of us in the West have been taught that feminine energy is about giving."
>
> *~Dr. Eve Agee*

As I continued this deep internal inquiry, I also became aware that I had been trying to take care of and please everybody else but me, and was trying to be perfect in every role I thought I should play. For so long I have been on a path of wanting to be "good"—the perfect daughter, the perfect friend, the perfect student always at the top of my class, the perfect sister, the perfect aunt … and I had totally lost myself.

I was exhausted and ready to embrace my feminine.

Each morning when I found myself sitting in front of the ocean, I incorporated healing chants for the waters, and I drummed for the waters. As I continued these healing practices, I noticed a certain responsiveness of the ocean, a communication, of sorts, between us.

I started to receive messages of fluidity and pure femininity. I would send messages and chants of love, and the waves would come close to me and caress my feet, bringing me insight and wisdom.

I started receiving even more messages: direct downloads of rituals, practices, and guided visualizations. I was receiving deep wisdom from the Great Mother Ocean—wisdom of remembrance, of the sacredness and power of the womb as a portal, of the feminine as a vortex of creation.

I started creating rituals, adding meditations to my daily practice of sitting in front of the waters of the ocean. I journaled about the waters of our bodies, our blood, our tears, our sweat …

THE JOURNEY

My very first journey into the landscape of my femininity was into my womb space—for healing, self-care, and direct revelation. I decided to take this journey with my medicine drum sitting on the beach with the waves in the background. I began drumming, bringing awareness down to my body. I brought in gentle movements in my upper body, with my eyes closed, allowing the drum to take me deeper, allowing a wave of relaxation to move from my head to my feet. I called in the directions: the east, the south, the west, the north, below pachamama, above pachatata, the direction of my own heart and the direction where I reach the still point.

The next step was to find an area on my body that was tense. I noticed that my solar plexus—the emotional energy center—was always contracted. My stomach was contracted, too. I seemed to be always sucking in my stomach because a flat stomach was considered beautiful.

As I witnessed my solar plexus, I honored its pain and sat with it. I called in my power animal to help me. I called in my higher self to drop a line of energy from my solar plexus down to the Earth. Inside of this internal journey I noticed a moon-like landscape with monolith phallic, jagged structures. I noticed a body of water in the distance with stagnant, still waters, like a swamp. I asked my higher self to show me an animal that represented me so that I might find out what was hurt on that animal and heal that part.

I saw a gazelle running on this landscape. This gazelle was running really, really fast—she was beautiful! Everything was perfect on this gazelle. She was light on her feet, graceful, and agile. I thought, "Perfect! Great!" There was nothing wrong with me because the gazelle looked perfect. Deep down, though, I knew that I had to look more closely, so when I looked at the gazelle I saw that her eyes were completely crazy. Her eyes showed her soul—she looked afraid and completely lost running around and not knowing where she belonged.

I asked my higher self to show me the part of my body that was like this gazelle: perfect on the outside and yet lost, afraid, and alone. The answer I received was that it was my *womb space*. My womb space was in the dark: lost, filled with fear, and abandoned without nurturance. I had never acknowledged it. I didn't know what to do with it. I had just never thought about it! My womb space was crying out to be acknowledged as a part of me. My womb was telling me that I was completely cut off from my innate power.

As I received this information from my womb, the landscape in my journey started changing, becoming an ocean with big waves and many birds. I received guidance to work with the ocean and her deep waters. I thanked my higher self and did a ritual in my journey to start the healing process of my womb space. I saw many animals during this journey including a white crocodile, a dragon, and a deer, and I was inspired to write a few words about the white crocodile.

I also made the commitment that every day I would sit with the great mother ocean to reclaim my womb.

White crocodile,
born out of the void of creation, from the deepest darkness of
ultimate consciousness.
What is darkness but the contrast to pure light.

White crocodile came into my life to teach me full acceptance of the realms we call "other," the realms of the void, the realms of the cosmos, of the primordial sound.
White crocodile is an ally of the highest order.

I am ready to explore her, to go deep, to seek, to see, to hear and to know. She is love and wisdom ancient. In its infinite love, Spirit opened my awareness to white crocodile.

You see, I had been afraid of the places in me where white crocodile could be found,
I was afraid of the places in me that could be dark and swampy.
The places in me where I had to look beneath the perfect surface,
the places where I had to sift through the programming.

White crocodile,
White iridescent scales
Shining softly
In the darkness of the deep cosmos
White crocodile, your teeth exposed
In a beautiful grin of love and mischief
Ancient mother
Ancient cauldron
Brewing, birthing
New ways of being
Teachings of new perception
White crocodile
Confident, brave in her uniqueness.
Accepting of herself, her infinite powers
Opening her soulful eyes, to invite you in.

I look deep in your amazing eyes and I see the whole universe reflected in them. I see the whole universe in its beauty and majesty.
I see me.

White crocodile and the sky dancing dakini.
The spiral of interweaving movements and consciousness,

the spinal rotations and full twists of flight.
White crocodile, standing on your strong back, I take flight and jump high,
I spread my wings like brother eagle and soar, and gently land on your
back again.
White crocodile
Ancient mother
Your wisdom is deep, as is your love.
Thank you
I love you
I love me.

RECLAIMING OUR CYCLES

Many modern women lack a clear idea of what femininity means. I believe
that no matter how you define your femininity—giving, receiving, water, fire,
moon, sun—the new Feminine Evolutionary is about reclaiming nurturance,
beauty, acceptance, wholeness, sexuality, inner radiance, creativity, intuition,
and divinity. Femininity is our ability to express ourselves and contribute at
the highest level, while claiming the sovereignty of our bodies, our visions,
our thoughts, and our creations—leading to pure ecstatic expression.

INVOCATION, RITUAL, CEREMONY

Being Love, remembering Love
The ocean dances
Expanded expression
Under the sun
Expanded presence
Ultimate ever-present witness
Deep holding of my womb
Woman awakening

Surrender is
Allowing the Universe, the divine to make love to me
Allowing myself to feel the pain of my wounds
Willingness to letting go, to stop holding
Letting the ocean take away the pain

Dancing with mother cacao, womb pulsing
The journey of discovering that I have the love of the universe
Embodying being the instrument of the Divine.

OCEAN: HEALING WATERS MIRACLE

One morning, at the end of my meditation with the ocean and the sun, I was guided to walk a few steps. When I looked down, there on the sand was algae that looked exactly like a womb with fallopian tubes—like a "grounded" womb. I had never seen anything like it in my whole life! I knew that I had to dive even deeper into this work.

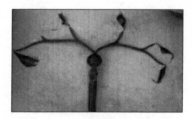

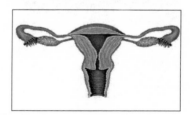

A DEEP YEARNING: HOW THE FEMININE BECAME MY SHADOW

I have worked on the fear of being me for a very long time. I have a deep desire, a burning thirst to step into my power, and yet at the same time am stopped by an unnamed terror of what will happen if I do. I become numb and stuck.

I have always had a deep yearning to fully be a woman—a Woman with a capital W. But, every time, I stepped into fear, perhaps fear of having "too much power" as a woman …

As my shamanic and energy practices grew, I started giving myself shamanic journeys to get into altered states of consciousness and track my shadow, to understand my journey as a woman, to finally be able to come home to my feminine essence.

In one of those journeys, I saw a vision of myself on my mother's breast, and thought, *I have to be strong, mom seems weak.* I continued to journey and have visions in order to track this. In another journey, I saw that when I was three or four years old, my mom was with her second husband and totally under his dominance, and I thought, *Not me, never.*

In another journey, when I was eleven or twelve, my mom was with her husband. He was violent, she wanted something he wasn't giving, and when she asked again he hit her. She didn't do anything, just sat there. At that moment, I thought, *Never, ever, will I put myself in place where I'm weak and can't defend myself.*

The feminine has been redefined over and over and over. But, I realized with dismay that *for me,* being feminine had become equivalent to the shadow aspect of me. The shadow is our deepest predator, those parts and layers of us we disown or don't think are acceptable—those parts of us that are undeveloped. I realized that I had equated "femininity" with self-defeating and self-sabotaging behavior. These are the words I had for my feminine: lazy, loser, not trustworthy, weak, inadequate, needy, silent, submissive, obeying, absent, "just sitting there" …

The *spiritual and energetic hysterectomy* I had given myself was present in all the areas of my life, even in how I interacted with people.

I remember a powerful interaction I had with a man named King. I had done something really great, and he said, "That's sweet." I remember starting to smolder in silent anger, thinking, *Sweet, sweet that's all he has to say!* Because, sweet to me meant weak or stupid, As I was getting angry, I caught myself in this judgment about the word *sweet.*

As part of my journey, I had promised myself to fully express myself, so I decided to be bold and ask Mr. King what he meant by "That's sweet." He explained that he was very touched by my gesture. This blew my mind, it brought me to the realization again of how much I had let myself believe in the pervasive collective beliefs about the feminine.

That night I decided to meditate outside. I was reflecting about that incident, and my thoughts drifted to pachamama, our planet, about the many times our planet offers us her sweetness. I was thinking about the scents of roses, cacao, ylang ylang, jasmine and even freshly mowed grass. I love those sweet scents; they always make me feel good and happy and at home. They are an integral part of the beauty and mystery of Gaia.

As I was looking up at the sky I was transported by the beauty of the stars and the earth and I decided to create a "sweetness practice" to accelerate my healing process. *I consciously allow myself to be and feel sweet.* From this, I have created the most magical scent—I imagine it as pure *shakti* and feminine life force. I wear it every day, and I notice that every woman who comes in contact with me asks about it. Their bodies (and mine) just come alive when they use it. I ask these women to encode themselves with words or symbols of self-love, tracing them with a rollerball of essential oil on their bodies. I call this scent "Maia of the Pleiades," because that is the star I was looking at when I decided to create a sweetness practice.

This period in my life of embracing the shadow and being a beacon of light has been the biggest challenge—to pioneer the state of fearlessness that I am upholding, not giving in to future fears, and following the path the universe has for me. I am allowing myself to be on my own sovereign journey back to the wholeness of my Feminine. To step up and follow what is true in my heart.

When I express myself with fearlessness and courage, unshackling everything that has been holding me back, my soul is ignited, and I feel uplifted and connected to Divine realms.

I invite you, Sisters, to allow this feminine essence and knowing into your own being—that by embracing your shadows you can become a radiant beacon of light for yourselves and others, allowing this light to shine bright and allowing the light of others to shine, as well. I invite you to be all that you can be, to be the Creatrix of your own life!

A'Ho!

Dr. Marie Mbouni, founder of Ecstatic Expression: Remembering Love, Sexuality, Sovereignty, and Success is a #1 Amazon best selling author, #1 International best selling author, full-spectrum healer of Shamanic and Energy medicine, womb wisdom alchemist, ceremonialist, and practicing medical doctor. All these techniques help her share her medicine, which is love. *Marie intuitively knew as a child that her destiny was to serve as a healer. She fulfilled her dream of becoming a doctor and practices as a highly regarded*  *and well-renowned anesthesiologist in Southern California. Online, in person, and at retreats, she guides those called to serve at all stages of their development, from the very beginning of their calling to those at the top of their game. She offers transformational experiences for changemakers and leaders wanting to step into their power and purpose and for women leaders ready to step into their deep feminine wisdom. Her clients tap into the spiral of consciousness, energy, intuition, creativity, and heart centeredness to create certainty, clarity, and knowingness. To become radically empowered from within while being deeply held, to get more done with less stress and to live holistically in balance, harmony, love, joy and interconnectedness. She firmly believes that her mission and Soul purpose is to help her clients say YES to their full ecstatic expression. A life fulfilled! Marie can often be spotted painting while singing out loud on her terrace. Learn more:* **www.mariembouni.com**

Dancing with Grace

BY CIA MOORE

As I sit down to write these words, I bow my head in devotion, gratitude, and love. I ask to be of service to the greatest good of all. I offer myself as a clear channel through which Grace can enter and speak. I feel my womb begin to expand with breath and inspiration. My toes and hands are tingling and the crown of my head feels like a flower blossoming and opening as a golden, nectarous love pours in letting me know that Grace is here. Simultaneously, my heart is pounding and I feel resistance. I feel fear in allowing these words to flow. My mind comes in, second guessing myself and asking "What if I can't do this? What if I'm not good enough?" I hear the thoughts streaming through my mind and I choose to not believe them. I know that if those thoughts exist then the opposite thoughts also exist. "What if I can do this? What if I am good enough?" Or maybe I can let all thoughts go, surrender, and listen deeply to the silence of my heart.

I take a deep breath into my heart, knowing and trusting that Grace, like a Divine Mother, lives at the very center, holding me in an all-inclusive embrace saying "I am here. Come home to me. Trust in me. Let me hold you and I will carry you through." As I sink deeper into this loving embrace, I am held and supported. I remember and know I am home.

Eight years ago I experienced a life-changing moment of Grace. I was deeply unhappy. I hated myself. I was tired of hurting myself and others wherever I went. I didn't want to live anymore. I didn't know what to believe and I was scared to go on. I was on a walk one day and found myself falling to my knees, begging and crying "I'm done. Please take me. Please teach me how to live a life of service to the greatest good. Please teach me to be a loving person. I'll do whatever it takes. I don't know how to love. Please teach me." Then I stood up and continued walking.

This moment wasn't exciting or grandiose. It was simple and effortless. It was Grace. Within a couple of months I began hearing a stream of negative thoughts about myself running through my mind, but I didn't believe them. I began to ask myself "Who is the 'I' that doesn't believe the thoughts running through my mind?" This was the beginning of my awakening. This was the beginning of discovering that which I am, or more accurately said, that which I am not.

Within a year of that moment, I found myself flat on my back for four months with a back injury. This injury was another way that Grace showed up in my life. I spent those four months examining and questioning my mind. Some days were torture, other days were filled with curiosity and exploration. During this time, Grace taught me how to surrender and allow the mind to be what it is without identifying with every single thought that streamed through. Grace taught me how to love my mind and reprogram it with loving thoughts. I began to heal physically. I began to attract the appropriate healers and spiritual teachers into my life to support me in my journey. I began to unwind thirty years of trauma that was locked in my body.

In 2011 I attended a five-day silent retreat. This is where Grace made another big appearance in my life. On the second day of the retreat, I experienced a death of the idea of a personal self and will. I was extremely disturbed. I felt as though someone told me that my child was going to die in five minutes. I felt deep pain and grief. After twelve hours of seeping in this grief, I broke down crying. As I cried, it felt as though my heart busted open and the most beautiful, all-inclusive energy flowed from it and wrapped me in a warm, loving embrace. I was completely held and supported. When I opened my eyes there was nothing left but this all-inclusive, loving Grace. I knew myself as the One awareness looking through everyone's eyes. With no separation, I felt complete intimacy with all of creation. I knew myself as the One infinite space from which all things are born. There was no longer a search—no fear. There was no other, just a simple, loving, all-inclusive Grace.

I laughed at the simplicity of Truth. It's all right here, right Now. There was nowhere to go and nowhere to be. I experienced each moment as a divine gift and honor. I experienced the self from a place of no self.

Grace comes with a knowing that all is always already forgiven. Grace seemed to bestow Her gifts upon me, yet there's also a remembrance that the gift of Grace is not new but has always been here. Grace is often defined as something bestowed upon us without having to earn it, yet how can we earn something that we already are? Grace is also defined as simple elegance or refinement of movement. I love this. I experience Grace as a flowing current that carries me effortlessly when I let go of control and surrender into it. I also experience Grace through challenges that I may bump up against and move through in order to be refined. Like water, Grace is fluid. The less I resist the flow, the more elegant the dance.

When I heard the words "Grace is courage under pressure," that resonated with me. I experience Grace as living in the unknown, which often requires courage under pressure. The pressure is where the refinement comes in, the courage is the moment that opens the door to Grace. As I surrender my personal will over, I become aligned with the higher will of Grace.

I wake up in the morning, bow my head in devotion and ask, "How may I be of service today?" This question puts me into a "we" consciousness rather than a "me" consciousness. Being in "we" consciousness allows me to feel myself as part of a greater flow that I surrender into and this flow expresses through me, as Grace, in service to the Whole. This is how I surrender into the unknown and let go of control.

> Letting go of control and being lived
> by Grace is an experience of
> all-inclusive Wholeness.

When embodying an experience of all-inclusive Wholeness, there is no other. While I still experience the physical sensations and resistance of fear, there is a remembrance and knowing that there is no *other* to fear. If there is no *other* to fear, then to what am I having courage up against? Asking this question creates a Spaciousness that I can relax into, while allowing myself to feel the fear and resistance in my body, and move forward anyway. This leads to having an experience of having courage while under pressure, but from a place of knowing there's nothing to fear.

When I experience fear and resistance, I find that showing up in total honesty is the way to navigate through it. When I am showing up in total honesty and expressing from my inner Truth, Grace shows up at the same moment that I do. However, there is a moment of fear that I must have courage to walk through. It's a lot like being willing to walk through a fire and being so afraid to take that first step, with my heart pounding out of my chest, but once I do, I am completely held by Grace and don't get burned. I walk through the fire with Grace. Grace flows through me and as me, filling me with a deep sense of Truth and connection. I witness myself doing that which I was afraid to do, and somehow it's graceful and flows effortlessly with results more beautiful than I could have ever imagined on my own.

I experience this way of being as effortless. I am taking the action presented to me, walking through any fear and resistance, and I am completely held and supported. Sometimes showing up can feel like being asked to jump off the edge of a cliff. Grace is like a Divine Mother, with her arms spread wide open, at the bottom of the cliff saying "Trust me and I'll catch you," but I can't see Her. She asks that I trust in Her so deeply that I have the faith and courage to jump off the edge anyway. She catches me every time. With each jump, I learn to trust Her more and more.

In my experience, the trust doesn't change whether or not Grace will catch me; the trust changes my experience of the fall. The more I choose to jump with courage and faith, the more my trust builds and I learn to let go and fall into Grace, gracefully. Once I fall and allow Grace to create through me, Life seems to orchestrate a beautiful symphony that I get to be an instrument in and my story becomes a song more beautiful than anything I could have planned or imagined. I become a way for Grace to dance, sing, and create in simple elegance and refinement.

> It's a divine love affair between Spirit and
> form and I am the bridge through which
> they come together in total communion.

My current life situation is an example of Grace living and creating through me. My life has been turned upside down, or right side up, depending on how I look at it. The foundation that my life was once built upon is no more and I'm building a brand new foundation from scratch. I'm living in the unknown and I've never been more certain that I'm exactly where I am supposed to be.

Six months ago I was summoned to jury duty. I felt a huge resistance in my system around going to jury duty. I did not want to go, but I do remember thinking to myself and saying out loud "I feel like I'm going to meet someone there." My intuition was correct. I met a man. I immediately knew him to be soul family. I felt a deep, profound sense of familiarity and connection that I'd never experienced before. I was already in a committed relationship and engaged to another man, and was not looking to fall in love. I was honored to have made a new friend and felt blessed by his Presence. I had met a kindred spirit and was excited by the possibility of friendship and to be discovering soul family, which I had spent much of the previous year calling in.

Within a couple of weeks, it became evident that he and I were not just friends but deeply connected Beloveds who are meant to be together. I became clear that my most empowered path, in Grace and Truth, would be to follow this connection. I fought this within myself—I did not want this to be! I did not want to face the changes that I would have to face if it were true. I was living with another man who was supporting my children and I financially, and I loved him. I did not want to hurt him or face the fear of telling him the truth. I also hadn't worked in two years due to a back injury and I didn't have the resources or money to change my whole life around. So what were my options with this new man who had suddenly entered my life? Do I face this Truth or do I suppress it and hide from it? I had so many fears and "what ifs" swirling in my head. Having an affair and lying was not an option for me. Truth, alignment, and integrity were the only options. I knew that the only way to navigate this situation was with total honesty and integrity. All that mattered was that I listen deeply for my Truth and express and live from that place.

Grace has taught me that I don't need to worry about the how. I just need to have courage and show up in total honesty. I went to my partner and told him the truth. My heart was pounding out of my chest and it was one of the hardest moments of my life. It was also one of the most graceful moments of my life. I was held by Grace through it all. There was deep sadness, grief, and pain, but I felt supported and steeped in Love. He accepted the news with total Grace. He was angry and hurt, but held a deep respect for my being honest with him and did not lash out in anger.

We cried. I was blown away by the love that could be experienced and expressed, even within such a painful event. Showing up in total honesty, no matter how hard it is, gave space for Grace to flow through and bless the situation with a sense of connection, gratitude, and love. I felt like a liberated diamond cutting through all illusion and only Truth came through this voice. It isn't pain free, but it is freedom. The events that have transpired since have been inspiring. My previous partner and I are uncoupling and shifting form from romantic partners to great friends. There are definitely painful moments, but for the most part, we are both experiencing Grace throughout this journey together. We are more honest with each other than we have ever been and our transition is being supported.

Now I find myself in the midst of my previous reality unwinding and a new one forming. Everything that was once considered my stable foundation has crumbled. I have no idea how I'm going to be able to support myself and my children on my own, but I am showing up each day, in total honesty, trusting in Grace. So far, each step of this new journey has unfolded organically and gracefully with many synchronicities that give confirmation and validation that I'm on the right path. I take action as it is revealed to me and I am continually delighted by how supported I am when I show up, work hard, and live honestly.

How do I know if I'm showing up in total honesty? I sit quietly, with my hands on my womb, and I listen. I enter my womb space, breathe into the center of my heart and I ask for my Truth to be revealed. I wait and allow the Truth to come to me. I approach my thoughts with a curiosity and question whether or not they are true. Being curious, and questioning my thoughts, creates a spaciousness that allows me to choose which thoughts I want to respond to and which ones I want to let go of. When I pay attention to my thoughts in this way, I see that I am not my thoughts, but the awareness of my thoughts.

> Being Awareness is being Stillness. Being Stillness is being the blank canvas through which Grace creates from. Grace is Truth.

As I listen in Stillness, my Truth is revealed to me through a feeling, a vision, or a direct knowing. I become aware of the next step, or action, on my path and I take it while remaining in integrity and expressing from Truth.

I know when I am living in Grace because my breath is expanded and flowing, synchronicity abounds, and I experience an inter-connectedness and intimacy with all that is. Grace allows me to be exactly as I am with no judgment. I experience myself from a place of neutrality where nothing is personal, but everything is felt. When I allow all of my humanity, from the darkest depths to the lightest heights, to be felt, experienced, and expressed, I feel ecstasy.

Ecstasy is zero resistance to *what is.*

Grace is *what is.*

Cia Moore is a Soul Artist, express-ing her inner world, spiritual journey, and healing through visual art. Her womb is a womb of creation, serving as a portal through which creativity is realized, experienced, and born. Cia is Wholeness birthing through her life experience in love, service, and devo-tion—and she loves it! Learn more: ***www.ciamoorelove.com***

HerStory

BY PHOENIX NA GIG

As we spiral into planetary catastrophe, the earth's heartbeat is pulsing beneath our feet and in our hearts. She, like us, simply can't and won't take any more. The unseen everything is waking up. The mass ritual abuse of women and children can no longer be ignored; we have reached a global psychopathy and women are rising. *She* is rising. But what is *She*? And why now?

A most beautiful and profound awakening is happening, a 21st-century re-evolution that's both political, philosophical, psychological, social, and educational. This is a revolution for all, and it's intimate, personal, embodied, and natural. It's sensual, wild, and pure. Perhaps it was 40,000 years ago that a woman first threw down her stone grinder and said, "Fuck this shit. I'm off." Perhaps it was Eve when she realized that she would be blamed for the pain and suffering of all of humankind. Truth be told, we will never know, because history missed a vital voice, a crucial record that is scratched and hard to hear, and is now screaming in our ear: *HerStory*. Without it, we are experiencing the annihilation of ourselves, each other, and the planet.

Feminism is *much* more than we think.

The Suffragettes fought for our equality with man socio-politically, bringing us (eventually) the right to vote. But *equality* is still a distant dream. Let us not forget it was still legal for a husband to rape his wife in the UK as late as 1991. We have the house, the car, the kids, the holiday, the education, and the vote … because we're worth it. Right? Apparently not. Deep inside a woman's body, her emotions are telling another story. All is not actually well in wonderland. *HerStory* is emerging, birthing through her deepest grief, the shiny billboards, the plastic tits, the botoxed faces, the vajazzled vaginas, and, oh my dear sister, through the deepest depths and beauty of our tears and our aching, broken hearts.

By day, woman may be fine. She may also emotionally reject—even loathe and detest—her every living cell. If we could hear the voice in the collective mind of woman today, what would it say? I invite you to listen. In her striving to live a good and decent life, we hear the ache and continual longing for a perpetual *somewhere over the rainbow*. We find ways to avoid the internal and existential angst of this moment of our existence that we are in now. Caffeine, sugar, eating, *not* eating—we get our fix in a variety of ways. It cannot be denied as we look around the streets, the sense of walking and talking in a Prozac nation: Women seem like clever, moneyed, living dolls. Eat, don't eat, look like this, don't look like that. Do anything but *stop and be* and feel into who and what you really are—let alone reach out to love and connect with another human being. And woman keeps quiet about it—*See no evil, hear no evil*—"No, nothing wrong with me."

Her hair and eyeliner is on straight, her kids are dropped at school, she goes to work, her hormonal implant is in her arm … could it be that an almost Orwellian nightmare is here? Woman has been trained to be either polite and politically correct or a cat-ass bitch, anything to avoid the truth of how she feels. Boys don't cry … and neither do we. We've manned-up our emotions—our body cycles and rhythms too—and have spent a lifetime mimicking the men with which our Suffragette sisters fought so hard to create equality. We have done the most extraordinary job of hauling ourselves out of old-style domesticity, controlling our hormones, and proving that we can do everything that he can. And, Sister, we *are* brilliant.

But on the surface a woman has had to adhere to certain codes of conduct and collusions with a culture obsessed with her repressed sexual energies and a want to dominate her body as a capitalist product to consume. Every one of us has participated in this internally and externally. With instructions on how to make "love," how to raise our children, how to eat, how to dress, and how to conduct ourselves in a stifled, emotional field, even the most awesome and empowered woman has had to block the sacred nature of her body to even exist. A woman's innate Sacred Feminine cycle has been repressed and labeled as dirty and a curse. Many wonderful women don't even know their cycle as anything more than a biological inconvenience or, even to a liberal feminist, an embarrassment. Woman is afraid to age, mature, or become all that she is, lest she be deemed worthless, unattractive, or damaged goods.

The homogenization of the individual to prepare her for the working world has led us to override a vital piece—we have blocked *Her* out. We've blocked out—with our busy and brilliant minds—the simplicity of our nature, our Earth, and the intelligence of our body to thrive with total connection to our self, our loved ones, and the planet. If the numbing of a woman's feelings is rooted in an essential disconnection with herself and her body's rhythms, if the ache and pain of billions of women over generations is alive in our bodies now and felt every month as pre-menstrual tension, anxiety, hysteria, and depression, then a new feminism is needed. But how, when the intelligence of that natural design within us is invisible? How, when today's humanity is born into fluorescent strip-lit rooms to mothers drugged up and on their backs?

The Sacred Feminine is rising. What is the movement, and why is this one any different from the one that many people scorn?

Sacred Feminine Evolutionaries are learning to plug back in to their nature. In their reconnection, they are healing their emotional realm and bodies and are beginning to shine and radiate with grounded, rooted, sensual wisdom, and gifts. They're still mothers, artists, teachers, doctors, lawyers, entrepreneurs—hell, we need this stuff in the White House! But, uh-oh, as her menstrual cycle kicks back in, that's right ladies, when a woman plugs back in and her lights switch back on, guess what? She'll experience a broad range of good-feeling emotions as she returns from the dead, but she'll also be pretty pissed off about having lived an existence without it. Who and what took one of her fundamental natural birthrights away, and why is her rage about it not welcome in the world ... so not welcome that her own gender rejects her courage?

When we begin the journey to evolve deeper, we look within and begin to realize that, like the Earth, we have been raped, plundered, abused, dismissed, and ignored. Our emotions and expression of that abuse are a revolting inconvenience to many in the banal landscape of a normal working day.

Sister, I know a secret. Sister, you are Sacred, you are Divine. You can be profoundly ecological, alternative, mindful, spiritually connected and conscious ... But all that has SO much more meaning the moment when we drop our masks and roles together, when we bring all that we are to soften into the deepest darkest divine, when our inner temple opens, and we hear the belly of the earth, the wind, the wilds of nature whispering our names again. Sister, together we remember again that we are innately wild—interconnected with this earth and all creation.

If I said you were a Goddess, you'd hang up the phone.

But if we said that the gifts of your beautiful body, your cycle, and your menstruation were for a period of *tens* of *thousands* of years on this planet at the *center* of certainly not all but many tribal earth-based communities (across all of Africa, Australia, and Neanderthal Europe and some tribes still today)—you might be curious.

If we said that the power of your moon time was so respected that every male hunter respected with awe the solidarity of the women who walked painted in Red Ochre and blood—dancing, singing, and drumming—then you might feel a shift in perspective and be able to apply it to modern life.

If we said that women had the gift to talk to all of Nature, to hear the voices of plants, animals, ancestors, and spirits through her cycle, to ensure the balance and harmony in the community, then you may start to feel energized.

If we said that her sensuality and her sex was the most beautiful expression and radiant gift in life, you may just put this book down and go outside and dance, and you might just quit your day job and start to journey deep within.

And if we could imagine a world where we could bring that depth of beauty and presence to our everyday lives as mothers, artists, entrepreneurs, lawyers, teachers, nurses, doctors ... then the dream can begin for real. That new consciousness can flow into your personal purpose as fuel for something so much greater, both personally and collectively.

If we said that we know there have been periods of tens thousands of years where there was *no rape,* where there was *no abuse,* that in us is the memory and the potential of a time when women were free, and that that time has not been seen since but *will* be seen again ... then Sister, who are you, and what could you be?

What happened the last time you cried in public? Would you even dare to do that, let alone rage and scream how you really might feel? What is this rejection of the feminine body? If your guts turn with revulsion at the mention of the word *woman*—let alone womb, blood, menstruation, menopause, matriarch, menarche or crone—*you are not alone*, join the club. Feel the revulsion, because it takes feeling it to dare to begin to address it. And if it feels like that for *women*, imagine what it's like for men to try to understand, let alone feel.

The truth is this: In our womb we carry the most fertile gifts. When we untame ourselves and free the emotionally locked, chained, shackled, and shamed aspects of woman within, we begin to feel once more. We feel this earth. Her heart. Her breathing. Her cry for *no more*. We feel a collective heartbeat, and her knowing laps our shore. Slowly we awaken and begin to ripple with earthly delight.

When a woman drops her awareness deep down, bringing her conscious awareness from her mind down to feel her soul, down to the center of her *womb*, she becomes aware of an inner magic. She discovers an innate gift to feel deep into her heart and to flow effortlessly into a dance with all of life.

Woman discovers that she has a conscious connection with her womb that is akin to a sacred center at the heart of her body. No church, no dogma, no science needed. Harnessing this awareness, she gathers deep intelligence from her body's wisdom—of her life, her environment, and the acknowledgment that the earth herself moves with this sacred feminine energy. In her reconnection to her cycles, a woman discovers that her menstrual time and her menstrual blood are powerful in bringing her strong grounding with the earth. Her blood returns as the natural conductor in her body to drop her awareness down to the earth and in an almost mystical, meditative state harness powers of deep sensing, visioning, seeing, feeling, and creative gifts.

If you do not have a temple—they're not so common these days—and if you haven't been raised by an ancient lost culture, beginning the journey to remember and reconnect with your womb can be a challenge, especially without any guidance. Our mothers, aunties, sisters, and grandmothers have been alone, too. But this journey can be luscious, abundant, sometimes painful, deep, and at times richer than any feast or throne that the civilized world can bring. Your wild woman speaks to you through intuition, feelings, sensing, and dreams. A woman's cycle and menstrual blood returns as the natural conductor of her body, and *whoa*, guess what? It connects her to the moon.

Once honored, once worshiped, once adored. We are seeing HER rising once more in fierce connected love to birth grounded, connected, feeling, bleeding, womb-centered women ... and with this grounding in woman's bodies reharmonize the loss and annihilation of our humanity here on Mother Earth.

This wisdom is more powerful than anything outside of us. When we listen to it, we know we are more powerful than we could possibly imagine. We are united, we are woman, we are the earth. And She is listening, speaking and calling us home. If we exercise the right to express, protect, and feel using our womb ... if we vision, dream, feel, and create from this sacred life center ... we're talking about an awakening of the Sacred Feminine. What that looks like is up to us—all of us. The Sacred Feminine is fierce and sexy, because this stuff is where it's at. Who's it going to be? Well love, it's going to be me, and, I hope, it's going to be *you*.

The Hopi elders had a saying: "You are the one you have been looking for."

I know that whispers to me.

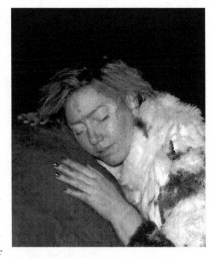

Living in the wilds of Dartmoor, England, **Phoenix Na Gig** *is The Womb Whisperer, offering women a drop into the oceanic mystery of womb magic and medicine. With a deep connection to womb, earth intelligence, and the wild and sacred language of the feminine, Phoenix holds one-to-one Womb Whispering Ceremonies—transmissions of a woman's deepest sacred womb wisdom guidance and remembrance of their erotic, juicy, interconnectedness with all of life. Phoenix Na Gig's academic research thesis in the "Anthropology of Menstruation as Sacred, Ritual and Divine Experience for Women" is nourished by the hundreds of women she connects with worldwide through the belly of Mother Earth bringing through a sacred vision of earth, women, and our humanity. Learn more:* **www.wombwhisperer.co.uk**

The Rise of the Sovereign Mother

BY TARA PRESTON

Motherhood was a spiritual initiation for me that ushered in greater evolution of my soul path.

The birth of my firstborn was not only a catalyst for living more of the life I felt called to live, but also an awakening of the goddess in me. Shortly after that came the searing pain of a world I felt did not always honor the feminine.

A few years later I would see myself blossom into a woman who would love herself more deeply than ever before. I would begin to embrace not just the aspects of myself that I enjoyed but also the aspects that I once hid from the world. I released years of shame from a difficult childhood, allowing me to free myself from playing small. A slow awakening through the next few years of this motherhood initiation would uncover a deeper soul's calling and a more authentically, self-expressed version of the woman I was born to be.

It was by embracing the transition into motherhood that I had then opened to a well of deep wisdom and radiant inner beauty. This was something I sensed was present but had never connected to before. Through my twenties I would touch on this inner world but never fully immersed myself into the depths of it.

Prior to becoming a Mama, I was a professional make-up artist and prided myself on my ability to see the beauty in other women. However, that was definitely not always the case for myself.

For years I worked with high-end cosmetic brands that focused on flaw-less skin, current fashion trends, and a conception of beauty as perfect. Even-tually I felt contained within this limited idea of beauty, and I longed for the freedom of imperfection that celebrated rather than concealed.

The year leading up to the birth of my daughter I could feel myself stretching the edges of my old life. There were so many pieces that no longer fit the woman I could sense I was becoming, and the narrow view of the beauty industry was another one of them.

Once she was born, my heart continued to fill with so much love for the growing little girl in my presence. At the same time it became clear that my old life no longer felt like me. I was unsettled. I felt an inner stirring. There was a mourning taking place within me that I hadn't fully acknowledged but was beginning to sense. I was starting to feel lost between new and old aspects of myself, and on top of all of that I was learning to hold my center in a whole new way.

Earlier in my twenties after I left a broken home, I discovered the Moon's healing power, and began flowing with her cycles. As I connected to the cycles of the moon at various stages I could feel layers of old pain wash away. As a young woman, I had felt abandoned and lost. Over the course of a few years, I would cycle with Moon. She took me deeper and deeper into myself until eventually I felt more connected again, allowing a new me to emerge. Through this process of self-healing, I had reclaimed parts of myself that I had disconnected from through painful childhood experiences. Who I was becoming through this process was much more aligned to my true self.

Somehow I knew that if I fully embraced what I was opening up to at this juncture of life, that a deep life transformation was at hand. I knew that the Grandmother Moon was my companion as I began to shed, heal, reclaim, and rebirth once again.

As I started to realize the profound change that Motherhood was initi-ating, I began to pay attention. I let go of certain aspects I could feel I was beginning to shed.

As a new mother I felt deeply, just as I always had. For the most part, I viewed life below the surface. I had explored the healing arts for years (but was still hiding my spiritual self) prior to leaving the beauty industry and had self-healed many layers of my own childhood wounds through my jour-ney with the Moon.

A year into my new journey as a mother I could clearly see how my perspective was different than most. As an awakening mother I felt I had a unique perspective on what I sensed my daughter needed to thrive. I wanted to nurture my own child in a way that felt different from many of the current views around me. As far as I could see, there was no current system, like a daycare or other childcare provider, that would do a better job than myself. These were important bonding times for me. I wanted to create a connection that nurtured a deep feeling of safety in the world for my daughter—and the necessity of my own presence in those early years was a big part of that.

My husband was moving through his own initiation into parenthood. He was feeling the pressures of being a provider and was finishing his MBA and wasn't always fully available to hear the deeper concerns of my Motherhood initiation. This often-activated abandonment issues that would tailspin me into mild depression. In fact, the demands were taking a toll on both of us. The modern-day city rat race left us feeling disconnected from a supportive tribe.

I was growing unhappy and yearning for a space in life to reinvent myself once again. I was feeling called to live in the safe arms of Mother Earth and cultivate a real rhythm that would support me to live in a way that felt sustainable not just for me but for my family as well.

I could no longer deny the deep desire to live a life that supported my soul path as a fully awakened mother. I wanted a life that supported the emerging sense of who I was becoming as a sacred woman *and* as a mother.

On top of all of this I was feeling the rise of deeper wounds that I had never felt fully before being activated at the core of my being. My unique perspective around parenting had yet to be truly refined, so my voice as a new mother was sometimes lost in the traditional role of motherhood and old cultural programming that wasn't in alignment with who I was being called to be. I knew there were aspects that did not work for me: Why didn't I want my child to sleep alone in a crib? Why did daycare not work for me? Why did so much of the popular child rearing advice not ring true for me? Why didn't I want to return to a 9-to-5 job?

Eventually, intuitive parenting became my go to, but it often felt like further isolation from the world around me.

As my discontent for my current life set in, I would try to open up dialogue around new solutions to support my spiritual path and new motherhood. I often felt my husband didn't understand—even though he tried—how we were going to navigate this vision, especially when I couldn't find any real-world examples of anyone living this way. I was frustrated at the lack of support around my effort to express what I felt was needed for our evolution as a family.

But a new vision of myself as a divine awakened woman was emerging.

I didn't know exactly who she was yet. But I knew that I didn't want my daughter feeling lost in the confusion of a society that didn't seem to always honor the path of the heart.

As a spiritual guide for my daughter, I knew I didn't want to just tell her how to really be the woman she came here to be if I didn't feel like that myself. I knew I had to become that woman so I could be that soulfully embodied guide for my daughter. I knew then that I was not willing to sacrifice the desires of the woman I was being called to be at that time. I knew that taking a stand for her truth, higher vision, and empowerment was the biggest gift I could ever give my daughter.

I had no idea how this would unfold.

In truth, I thought this spiritual adventure into the unknown would be so much easier than it was. As someone who had already experienced a rather tumultuous childhood, I knew I was up for the challenge but was in no way prepared for the unraveling that came after.

As I said yes to more of my sacred path, more rose up to be healed, cleared, and realigned. So much of this period of life often felt like the dark night of the soul. Wound by wound I was asked to heal stories of abandonment, low self-worth, poverty consciousness, and lack of self-love. That healing was indeed accelerated once I learned how to lean into the gifted guidance of the women mentors who I would later find.

For weeks, I cried in secret. It wasn't just my own wounds being exposed, asking to be healed, it was a deeper mourning as well. Everywhere I looked I felt an abandonment of the feminine. I felt deeply the mistreatment of Mother Earth, how we had raped and taken from her without respect and leaving such a detrimental imbalance. As I began to feel into my unique feminine perspective I could feel the voices, gifts, and hearts of so many missing in the collective tapestry not only in my community but in the world.

At that time I began to feel an intense desire to return to a natural way of living. I felt a desire to live more fully from my heart, and I yearned for the rhythm and groundedness of Mother Earth. For me, city life made that difficult, and the looming return to a 9-to-5 job didn't support how I wanted to parent. All this left me feeling desperate to understand how I would navigate the journey ahead in a way that would support all of these newly uncovered facets of myself.

My healing began with a move to the country. This move gave me the space and connection time I longed for. My daughter was still small, and I used this time to nurture her, our family unit, and myself as well.

Before this move I was always on the go, pushing to create a life that really never honored my Mama values of rhythm and space to nurture my inner world. The city demanded it of me. Motherhood demanded it of me. My husband demanded it of me. But inside of me, amidst all of that constant *doing,* was a beautiful feminine essence that was dying to lead the way into a life that fully expressed of all parts of myself.

My husband is a beautiful man who always has led with his heart and highest intention for our family. We had never been conventional. Even so, when I awoke to a higher vision for our family it was challenging for both of us. I believe the deeper fear for him was whether I would be able to create a prosperous life by following this deeper call. There was sometimes a hesitation in following where my feminine heart was leading us, which meant that he wasn't always open to hearing why I was wanting what I was wanting or the pain that I was feeling around denying this part of myself. Given where we were at as new conscious parents he did the best he could, but often I felt misunderstood and not fully supported in my quest to follow my sacred path.

At this same time, I was nowhere close to having healed my money story. I leaned on him to figure that piece out for me, and this strained our relationship even further. I put pressure on him to provide for me past what he felt safe doing. And there was often confusion for both of us around traditional values in our society. Was it really possible to land on our two feet through something that seemed so different than so many people around us? There was nothing traditional about who we were dreaming ourselves to be.

Living in the country, I could more clearly hear my inner voice. My feminine nature began to find balance past the constant *doing* and *pushing* of my first years of motherhood in the city (not to mention the decade before that).

As I connected back into myself and back into the rhythmic pulse of Mother Earth, a gentle balance began to restore itself. For the next few years I would ebb and flow with the currents of the seasons and the cycles of the moon.

As I continued to awaken, various pieces inside of me danced around—pieces that wanted to be remembered, reclaimed, and more powerfully expressed. I so desperately wanted to be held at that time. How was I to navigate this unknown journey all alone? I began working with the moon yet again, but this time would it be enough?

I also began to feel the absence of the feminine in other everyday experiences. As I deepened my connection with Mother Earth I felt the sadness of destruction and the lack of respect for her resources. The beauty, creativity, and healing that the feminine brings felt lost and so undervalued in the world. Where were the gifts of the feminine being upheld in my community?

As a highly sensitive, creative, free-spirited woman, Motherhood continued to bring a rich experience of unconditional love for my child, but it also brought the pain of feeling deeply misunderstood. I had dreams for my child, but I also had desires of my own. The balance of cultivating my own sense of purpose, combined with parenting in a way that honored my feminine values (and free-spirited nature) left me often feeling suffocated in my expression.

I quickly discovered that putting everyone's needs before my own would only leave me sacrificing aspects of myself that needed to be nurtured for my own thriving authentic expression. Claiming space for my inner world to be nurtured became a regular practice. I brought into this self-connection time art exploration, prayer, energy healing, journaling, and other tools to center powerfully into my core. As I got to know myself even more, a deeper vision for my own sacred path began to emerge. I wanted to understand my gifts and how that contributed to my sacred work here on the planet.

The good news is I was getting closer.

I wanted to be a happy, thriving Mother—and that meant following my passion and uncovering my sacred path.

I wanted to be the Mother who could share with and model for her daughter the experience of what it means to truly live your purpose.

I wanted to be the Mother who trusted herself, honored herself, and courageously followed the call of her soul, so that one day I wouldn't have just talked about the miracles of living a heart-led life but that I would have actually done it.

The wounds of disconnect, abandonment, and loss that had been amplified after the birth of my daughter slowly began to heal with the wisdom and with medicine of these powerful feminine cycles. As I flowed forward, I began releasing the old pain of my feminine wounding, then eventually birthed a new me.

With every cycle I would deepen into more of who I was being called to be. My power hour became the cornerstone of this inner world exploration. My old life before Motherhood began to fall away, making these years in the country yet another powerful initiation. The balance of the cycles created a balance for my family life as well. The New Moon became a space for myself and family connection time, which often meant slowing down for beautiful periods of rest. The Full Moon was active, and I would often use that extra burst of energy to focus on my newly built passion-based business. I began to cultivate a nourishing rhythm that served my own path and the well-being of my family.

Years later as I began serving other women on this path, I would see over and over again how mothers are very often the spiritual catalyst for a shift in consciousness for the entire family. When mom's energy shifts into alignment with more of her authentic path, the entire family benefits. How this actually affects the family can feel unclear in the beginning. But as we say yes to more of our soul's desires, we very often begin a journey of energetic releasing that triggers a healing of the relationship dynamics within the family. As the old aspects release and core wounds heal, our vibration raises, in turn raising the vibration of the entire family.

When we follow the inner calling, do the inner work, and use our voice to say yes to our needs (and no to obligation), the entire family shifts to meet us at this new understanding of who we have become—and our true sovereign feminine essence can shine in her fully embodied power.

*Tara Preston is a beauty shaman, cer-
tified soul art guide, Akashic record
consultant, and intuitive business
guide-ess. She holds powerful space
for spirited women to be the visible
empowered goddesses they were born
to be. After over a decade spent in
the beauty industry as a model and
makeup artist, Tara weaves together
various transformational tools combined with ancient healing wisdom to
support women in creating a powerful
sacred self-image that ignites the path
to their highest purpose, then attracts*
*the relationships, life, and business their soul truly longs for. Tara helps her cli-
ents deeply connect to their intuition, inner beauty, and soul's vision by working
with their natural feminine cycles. She holds a space of love and non-judgment,
allowing women to feel safe as they go deep into those messy, imperfect places
inside themselves, recalibrating their life and work so that it nourishes them to
the core. Through her Glamour Goddess Coaching Program, Radiant Mama Rising Year-Long Business Mentorship, and the upcoming Intuitive Beauty Cleanse
Program, Tara assists her clients in healing deep collective feminine core wounds
and soul-level rooted patterns. She facilitates deep and transformational work
that enables her clients to feel free, powerful, and beautiful in the expression
of their purpose in both life and business. Learn more about Tara by visiting
www.sacredfemininepath.com, and download your free copy of "The Inner
Beauty Archetypes."*

Fierce Initiations: Standing in the Fire of Love and Transformation

BY ELIZABETH PURVIS

The moment of my greatest awakening came not in a ritual circle, or meditation, or women's gathering. It was not at a retreat, event, or mastermind meeting.

It was in the middle of a spring day, just steps outside of my home in Portland, Oregon.

My husband and I had been screaming at each other again. I was the parent on duty that morning; we'd been in each other's presence for barely five minutes when the dynamite went off. I'd stormed out of the house to take a walk, get some air and clear my head.

Except that I didn't clear my head. Instead, I got on the phone with a dear friend. An experienced transformational facilitator, he held space as I fumed, silently listening to the frustration spilling from my mouth.

Until finally, his voice cut through the blaze in my brain. He simply said my name.

Elizabeth.

And then: *I want you to hear me.*

At that point, my husband and I had been in couples counseling for over six months. It wasn't that we weren't getting anywhere—we were way too engaged for that. We were all in; we loved each other and trusted our therapist. But we've been at it for six months and neither of us was happy with the speed of our progress. Something had to give.

And then ...

Elizabeth, listen to me. I want you to hear me.

I woke up. At that moment, the real work began.

Coaches, practitioners, healers and change agents talk a lot about "doing the work."

The work of transformation. Shifting what asks to be shifted so we can step into our greatness. Transforming patterns, rewriting stories, healing the wounds ... embracing the truth of who we are.

I have been fascinated with transformation since I was a little girl. Were you to go into my room, back at age twelve or so, you would have found books on astrology, numerology and witchcraft (they were harder to find back then), *The Prophet* (nipped from my mom), Richard Bach (ditto), Louise Hay and *What Color Is Your Parachute?* You'd also find books of early urban fantasy—retellings of folk and fairy tales, full of mythical creatures sharing space with mortals in the modern world.

I've always had a thing for shapeshifters—girls who turned into birds or wolves and walked, invisible, alongside humans. Later, when I wrote stories and tried to get them published, they all contained shapeshifters.

I would fantasize about becoming someone or something else. Not because I wanted to get away from my life—though believe me, I deeply wanted to get away from my life. But because I knew I was so much more than the little box I'd felt myself in, the box that others had put me in.

Back then, I had no idea about boxes, and how we put ourselves in them.

I remained asleep throughout college, and then during my early training in magic and modern witchcraft. The lure of transformation was strong, but those early studies left me with more questions than answers. I didn't think of myself as having "core wounds" or being separated the Divine; all I knew was that *my life will be soooo much better when ...*

Later on, my more advanced studies in magic began to fill in the gaps. Still missing, however, was a teacher who could facilitate the growth I didn't know I needed.

By my thirtieth birthday, I found myself in the kind of tremendous pain that only comes from being wildly out of alignment. I realized that to make the massive shifts I wanted, I had to get into an environment where I would be fully supported to do so.

Enter the transformation industry. Coaches, healers, energy workers, shamans. Instantly, I recognized magic. I saw my chance to *finally* become who I was becoming.

This may sound like "Wizard of Oz" kind of story. *The power was in you all along, my dear.*

It's not. This is a story about what it really takes. Because it's one thing to realize that the magic was in you all along. Accepting it and living it is a whole other deal.

The real awakening, in my experience, is the stepping on *that* path. The path of laying down the endless distractions and going where that part of you that has a vested interest in your staying the same is absolutely not willing to go. The path of true freedom.

And that means walking through fire.

You might be saying, *yeah, yeah. Elizabeth, we've got to get over our shit. Isn't that the whole point of personal growth?*

To which I ask, dear Goddess … have you really gone there?

I ask because … I *thought* I had. I told myself I had.

Not even close.

What came next made everything that I had done before—the pain and confusion of not being on purpose, quitting a six-figure job, crashing and burning, healing my money story and the shame-blame-not-good-enough-game—look like a cakewalk.

The specifics of the work that started that day, with that phone call, aren't that important, actually. What's important is *your* work. But I will share a bit about it here, because it does speak to a part of our experience that is truly the foundation of our thriving as human beings … and yet it is still barely talked about.

······⊙ℓ☺······

From a very young age, I felt like an outsider. Of course, we all feel that way at one point or another. For me it started early, and came with the feeling of deep isolation in my own home. Being different. The other.

I was one of those kids who wondered if somehow she had been born into the "wrong" family.

Fiercely independent, with a vision for my life that my external world hadn't caught up with, I fantasized about leaving my old life behind. Finding my tribe. Finding where I belonged.

By the time I hit ninth grade I couldn't wait to go to college. I'd look out my window and think, *I've only got three more years in this place. Then I'll be on my own. Then I'll be free.*

But freedom from my childhood, when it finally came, didn't look as I had expected. I had friendships and sometimes truly intense relationships. But there was a part of me that was always looking for a way out. I told myself that I didn't want to be "boxed in." So when field hockey ended, the school year ended and then college ended, I moved on. Cut ties. *On to the next adventure,* I told myself.

Until one day I looked up and noticed that, with a few exceptions, I hadn't maintained my friendships with anyone from the past. *Surely that was normal,* I thought. *It's normal for our time together to come to an end, and we all move on.*

Besides, I have a deeply nourishing community right now. I lived in New York City. I had friends who were New York Times best-selling authors. I was dating one of the top writers of comics and graphic novels. I was training in magic with women I loved.

My husband and I met a few years later. It was instant connection, and within a couple of months both of us had broken off our current intimate relationships. The day after we finally met in person (it was a long-distance relationship), I told him, *I'd marry you tomorrow,* and I meant it.

It was a deep connection … while at the same time, I wanted to run. *He's too clingy, too intense.* Meanwhile, there was one wall in me that just wouldn't come down. Truthfully, I didn't want it to come down.

The wall was a big part of who I was.

And so we continued. Over time, our connection changed. I started my business and got on the path of purpose. We loved each other deeply. But the tension between us grew, and I chalked it up to "growing in different directions." I figured it was all just part of the journey. I was immersed in "personal growth" and yet was *completely* oblivious to how I was creating the same old story of isolation.

Then our baby came. And that's when things began to get weird.

The first week that we brought our daughter home, I was sitting in a chair with her in my lap, gazing down on her in the way that new mothers do. All at once I was hit with a wave of sensation.

The feeling of being alone as a child. Isolated. The other, in my own home. I remembered the feeling from being about eight years old.

The sensation was intense, paralyzing and shook me to the core. So distant, yet so familiar, and utterly de-stabilizing.

I have to get a handle on this. I have to be the mother now.

Eighteen months later, our relationship was at a breaking point. Sure, some of it was the stressors of caring for an infant, then a toddler. But there was something more. We could barely be in the same space without the kind of arguing that comes from utterly misunderstanding each other. He blamed me for everything, it seemed, instead of looking within. I looked within, shutting him out instead of communicating. Truthfully, I didn't really know how.

I knew something was very wrong, but we had a baby to take care of. We deeply enjoyed the time with our daughter, and our time as a family. But we struggled to find closeness.

Eight months after that, I went to work with a coach. A bombshell came out.

I said to my husband: *We need coaching!*

He said, *No, we need therapy.*

During the first months of counseling, we learned how to be together without setting each other off. Our love for each other was never a question. But somehow, we couldn't see each other as we were. I remember thinking that there was something inherent in our personal wiring that simply wasn't compatible.

And yet, we *were* compatible. I knew it without a doubt. Underneath it all, his essence—the man I fell in love with—was still there. The things that brought us together—the creative life, especially—were still there. How could this be?

Elizabeth, I want you to hear me. That book on adult attachment styles that I told you about. Did you read it? You need to read it. And then you need to talk to my friend who can help you.

That night, I downloaded the book to my Kindle, and there was my problem, laid out on the page. We were a textbook case of conflicting adult attachment styles. Our blueprint for relationships, including our coping mechanisms, completely clashed. His anxious attachment style triggered my avoidant attachment style. And we could barely talk without massive friction in our respective brains, resulting in countless explosive arguments.

A few days later, I raged at the therapist. *Why didn't you tell us about this before?*

I did, she said. *You just didn't hear me.*

Almost overnight, it became abundantly clear that my attachment style was the source of just about every challenge, problem or struggle I have ever had in my life. This is not hyperbole or exaggeration. The way we do relationships is the way we do everything. Your body, your money, your spiritual growth—everything is a relationship.

And I knew that if I didn't do the work to *truly* shift it—if I was not willing to leave the old way behind and learn to *be* the version of me with a secure attachment style—I would never become who I knew I was meant to be. I would continue to push away family, friends, clients, my husband and my daughter.

And I would probably die alone. This, after years of living, day in and day out, with the same sensation that had overtaken me in the early days of my daughter's life, the same sensation I lived with as a child.

The sensation of wanting so very hard to bond, but not knowing how. Outsider. Other. Alone.

I'll do whatever it takes, I told my husband. *I'll do whatever it takes.*

If any of this is ringing just a little bit too close to home, I have fantastic news. Your attachment style is adjustable. There are people who can help.

For the next six months I worked diligently with an expert in adult attachment who is also a master practitioner of neuro-linguistic programming (NLP), which he applies to attachment style. Our mission? To rewire my brain, as quickly as possible.

Now here's why I am telling you this story.

For six months I walked around in what priestesses call *a fierce initiation*. My brain was creating new neural pathways. Every single day, the tension between the "old way" and the "new way" was right up in my face. On many, *many* of those days, I walked around in a state of fight-or-flight—synapses fried, adrenaline running through my body. It was exhausting.

There were many, many days when I wanted to just hide under the covers. But I couldn't do that. I had a seven-figure business to run, full of clients with whom I have sacred contracts. I had a relationship to heal. I had a daughter. Life had to go on.

So even though most days felt like my brain was on fire and like I could have a meltdown pretty much any minute … I showed up. I put one foot in front of the other.

I stayed in the room. I stayed in the fire.

It was the hardest thing I've ever done. But also quite possibly the best, because I felt myself changing. Shape shifting, just like in the old stories.

Six months later, the feeling of isolation, of "other," that had lived in my body for so many years … was completely gone.

No trace. I can't re-create the feeling myself, like I used to. It does show up from time to time, at a fraction of the intensity, when I am under a lot of stress. But the old trigger simply does not exist.

That's the power of doing the hardest of all your work, no matter what it takes.

In our first session, my coach Gary told me that he could reasonably discern the attachment styles of celebrities by what they do in public. *I have never seen anyone with an avoidant attachment style with a huge platform, like what you want to create.*

I didn't do the attachment work for my business. I did it for my family. And for myself, so that I can experience the love and connection I desire.

All the same, it was a major aha—an answer to *why* I just couldn't break through certain aspects of my business. *Why,* after eight years, certain things were just not moving. It's because they couldn't move. Not in the old paradigm.

Now that I've truly said yes to my most significant transformation— the one thing I was most afraid to face—my true work in the world has begun. I have new programs, a new team, and a bigger community than I ever imagined.

......ᘒ......

Which brings me back to you, the new feminine evolutionary.

You've heard it before: if you want to heal and transform others, first you have to heal yourself.

I take a strong stand that none of us is broken. Our human systems are magnificent. All experience and behavior has a positive intention. Nobody needs "fixing."

What we do need, however, is more models of women who have made the choice to release everything that is not really them, and *become* who they truly are.

This, in my view, is the greatest and most urgent calling of the new feminine evolutionary. To do the work of transforming your deepest wounds. To face the BIG stuff, from a place of love and self-acceptance and most of all, radical self-honesty.

Think of what you desire for your life. Think of what you desire for your business. Think about how long you've wanted those things.

If you've been trying for those things for, say, eight years (as I was), and they are still not coming to pass … then there is a very good reason why. And it's time to get real.

Whatever you're avoiding is not going to shift on its own.

The one thing that will set you free is the one thing that your brain doesn't want you to see. The same is true of your clients and patients.

The expansion of the personal development industry over the past ten years is an astounding blessing. We have access to teachings, leaders and modalities that were unheard of even twenty years ago.

Paradoxically, that makes it even easier to hide out. In the seminar room, the virtual program, the retreat center in Bali, the Big Island or wherever the high-end transformational experience du jour is.

We all know that the global community is asking for a shift in consciousness. I believe our *modeling* will create that shift more than our teaching ever will.

This means saying yes to becoming a living example of the evolution—not from a place of "guru" but from that of global citizen and human being.

And that means truly doing the work, not fooling ourselves into believing that we are.

Of course, *you*, as evolutionary, are the sole evaluator of what "the work" is for you, and whether you're doing it or not. You are your own authority on this path.

I invite you to a whole new level of awareness, honesty and account-ability with self. An invitation to say YES to your next level of freedom, no matter what kind of fierce initiation it may be.

Here are a few suggestions for doing the work:

You always know. A key characteristic of the new feminine evolution-ary is radical self-honesty. We always know when we are hiding from something. A part of you knows. You may need some help uncovering it, but no one is going to tell you to do the work. Only you can do that. Be honest with yourself. You always know.

Find your why. Our patterns have a positive intention; they are always serving us in some way. Always. Today's limitation was yesterday's solu-tion. And yet, the brain has no reason to change. So you must find a reason. You must create urgency in yourself.

Stay in the room. I often hear clients say things like, *I need to do some inner work; then I'll be ready. I need to go on a retreat, then I'll be ready. I need to go journal, then I'll be ready.*

Despite what the personal growth industry would have us believe—go away (to a retreat/seminar/program) and come back—that's just not how it works.

Humans change by having a new experience. By making different choices in the moment, in the thick of it, in real time.

Shifting an attachment style usually takes at least a year, if not twice that long. I did it in under six months ... because I stayed in the room. I was wildly uncomfortable and wanted to quit. Instead, I kept living my life.

Do your work in real time, in real life. We are all being asked to step into our next level of evolution. This means facing the music, not hiding out.

Know when you're done. Growth is a tool, not a way of life—even when it is a way of life. It is a means, not an end. While there are many layers to the work, and there is always more work to do ... know when it's time to consider it complete.

You are not here to "work on yourself." You don't need fixing. You are not a project. You are whole and complete, here to live your life and be a blessing to others.

That's what the deepest personal growth work is for, you see. To become who you are becoming. Who you already are, and always were.

Elizabeth Purvis is a teacher of magic and manifestation to thousands of women around the world, leading them to develop their Divinely-given Creative Power, especially in the realm of money. She is the creator of Feminine Magic®, a set of practices for women to magnetize their deepest Desires, and the founder of The Feminine Magic® School of Manifesting, where she teaches a holistic system of manifesting known for its consistent, repeatable results. A priestess and practitioner of Western esoteric traditions for over twenty years, Elizabeth is also a master business coach and income breakthrough mentor. Using her systems, Elizabeth's clients and students have achieved phenomenal results, including quadrupling their incomes in just a few short weeks, multi-six-figure launches and more. Discover more of her work and The Feminine Magic community at **ElizabethPurvis.com.**

Where Is My Mother?

BY SHILOH SOPHIA

Have you ever had an experience where something occurs and you suddenly feel like a different version of self who recognizes the former self as an earlier version of you that you have now moved beyond? A flash of personal thunder?

The morning worship felt threatening. I wasn't sure *what* was being threatened; I just had a sense something went very wrong. I had prickly skin and all but no language for what I was experiencing. Emotional electricity lit up my insides like a thunder bolt. *What is this?* I wondered. *Rage? Fear? Despair? Betrayal?*

I was at church to give praise, but no praise was on my lips. My usually dancing hips were fixed, my usually up-raised arms were by my sides, unwilling.

Everything as I knew it was about change.

I trudged up the San Francisco hills home to California Street, huffing and puffing, my lavender dress sticking to my legs and shortening my stride. My brow was knitted into a hurricane cloud. I didn't say good afternoon to anyone. I stomped, a rebel ready to unleash herself in a temper tantrum of cosmic proportions. And—still—I had no language about what was coming over the horizon.

It was Mother's Day. Although unconscious of it at the time, I had an expectation that this open-minded gospel singing non-Bible thumping church would talk about mothers. Other churches might not, but this was liberation theology that celebrated having room for everyone. *Everyone* had to include women, mothers—right? not just include, but uplift? All the other down-trodden were heralded as those worthy of our service and tithes.

Here, we broke bread with outcasts, with homeless, with transgender people, with punks, with pimps, and with tech geeks getting high on this version of the culture club, many still reeking of last night's adventures.

I had been here coming to this church off and on for a decade, since I was thirteen. My mother, Caron, a poet, brought me to prevent me from being an uptight Christian—and she had done well by me in this, and in many things. I learned to dance in the aisles, and I had indeed been liberated from the confines of being judgmental.

But, on Mother's Day, there was no talk of mothers in any fullness. The lack of attention to mothers struck me with the start of this soul-thundering odyssey. Yes, the words "Happy Mother's Day" were said, and obligatory carnations were passed out. But no one had bothered to search scriptures to find a mother to talk about—not Sarah, Rebecca, Rachel, or Leah, not even Eve, the Mother of all Living. What about Mary—shouldn't we be wishing the Mother of God a Happy Mother's Day? There was no talk of mother earth, not the feminine part in "created in our image" in Genesis, not women's work in the church, not the women who risked their lives to be His fourteen great-grandmothers. No mention of them. Nope.

There were plenty of women in leadership, so I can't blame just the men in robes. It wasn't an intentional exclusion; it just wasn't considered significant enough to preach and teach about. But, for me, the absence of the feminine struck a soul chord and vibrated throughout my earthly form and on up to heaven.

> "A great wonder appeared in heaven: a
> woman clothed with the sun, with the moon
> under her feet and a crown of twelve stars
> on her head."
>
> *~Revelation 12:1*

When I was home, I centered myself in my fifth-floor studio, as if orienting myself to a new origin location. I looked out the bay windows across the city that I loved, and I looked down at my feet on the hardwood floors, and at the handmade lace and brocade bedspread my mother made me. My fist was not raised, by my face was as I peered through the floors above me and reached my gaze all the way to where the big dudes that I loved sat on their thrones dispensing justice in an unjust world.

An inquiry in surround sound unfurled and filled the room, reverberated and echoed from my deepest soul space. I felt fear mixed with anger. If I am honest with you and myself, I wasn't even really sure where it was coming from. I didn't identify as a feminist, wasn't in relationship with the Goddess, and had yet to really grasp the suffering of women worldwide. This cry didn't come from "information" I already had, but it was authentic, not just as reaction to patriarchy. Yet with this fire, there was also an innocence—I simply didn't *know* ... but knew enough to know something was very wrong.

With all the courage of a child asking their parent the impossible questions, I asked the Father and the Son directly. I felt I had the ears of the Holy Ones in my attention. Surely, they had to have noticed my upset.

Where is my Mother?
Where is my Mother?
Where is my Mother?

The question surprised me with the potent power. Followed by a swift sudden dawning of consciousness, almost like a light bulb overhead, I felt— as if I heard—a woman's voice answer: *"It's me. Your mother. I'm right here."*

It was Mama Mary. *All this time?* I wondered aloud. *You have been here all this time. My mother. I have found you?*

I didn't have a relationship with Mother Mary. So, when I asked, "Where is my mother?" it didn't occur to me that Mother with a capital M might even be Her! That is how far removed She was from my experience of being Christian. I knew she was Jesus' mother and had been told she was a nice girl who said yes to God, like we should do. But I wasn't reminded in any church, at any time, that She had said about herself: *"From henceforth all generations shall call me blessed."* Or that when She presented Her son at the temple, Her soul would also be pierced, sharing in the suffering. Ever notice how non-violent leaders who question the current establishment are often marked by authority for elimination? Such was the case with Mary's son.

> "This child is destined to cause the falling
> and rising of many in Israel, and to be a
> sign that will be spoken against, so that the
> thoughts of many hearts will be revealed.
> And a sword will pierce your own soul too."

~Luke 2:34-35

This pattern of wondering about "Her" went way back for me. My mom later told me that as a young child I asked if Jesus had come from a broken family like I did, since "they" talked only about a father and a son. The day of my Mary epiphany I crossed a threshold, and the door on "father-only" God closed with a chilling wind. For a time, I felt a bitterness in my heart, right alongside the new awareness that there was, indeed, a feminine within my faith who had been here all along, without whom Christ would not have taken on human form. After all, when we take communion, the blood—His Blood—is, Her blood.

A perfect storm hurled me into a new reality. I was ready to tear down large patriarchal buildings in a single bound. I experienced a sense of betrayal and fear. I wanted to explore this new relationship, but I had no idea how, absolutely none. I asked women I knew, but no one knew anything of substance about this blessed woman who gave birth to the one we called God, without a human father. Was this secret a conspiracy? It would take years, and years still, to unravel the rage and transform it into possibility. My fury wasn't directed at any one system or set of beliefs. Yet, I knew that She has been intentionally hidden from us. But why?

> "The woman was given the two wings of
> a great eagle, so that she might fly to the
> place prepared for her in the desert…"

~Revelation 12:14

I asked my Grandmother Helen about Mary, called the *Theotokos,* The God Bearer in the original church of my Fathers. She said: "Yes, I knew Her. She was always, just, there. Her image and story were a part of it." I asked her why she didn't tell me about Her. I asked her many times, but didn't really get to the answer I felt she had. At her death, I received her one icon of the

Blessed Mother Theotokos flanked by angels—where she is *central* to the story, not on the periphery. Where I go to church today, She is there, thread in hand. I go so I can see Her and sort out the rest that still disturbs my restless soul.

"Wisdom is justified of all her children."

~Jesus, Luke 7:35

The next morning after my fit of anger, I walked to work just like I always did, walking by a church I always passed. And saw Her there ... a marble image of a woman with hands extended, standing on the world, with a snake beneath her bare feet. I began to see Her many places, as if—yes—she had always been here. That week I went to the Mission District and bought candles of the Nuestra Senora Guadalupe, and I made my first altar. I was home in myself, although I had little to work with, yet. Not having Orthodox or Catholic background meant I didn't have any of the Mary stories in my consciousness besides the birth narrative and a few scriptures, which I began to search out for clues. I knew a great adventure in Her was before me, but I had no idea that it would take the rest of my life to travel.

"Listen, put it into your heart, my youngest and dearest son, that the thing that disturbs you, the thing that afflicts you, is nothing. Do not let your countenance, your heart be disturbed ... Am I not here, I, who am your Mother? Are you not under my shadow and protection? Am I not the source of your joy? Are you not in the hollow of my mantle, in the crossing of my arms? Do you need anything more?"

~Guadalupe's words to Juan Diego, 1531

At the time of this awakening, I was twenty-three, going to art school and working at a big corporate gig, climbing that ladder in my pink cowgirl boots, hoop earrings and red lipstick. The same week, I attended a wedding with my hot motorcycle-riding boyfriend, and the bride and groom were from Somalia. Looking at the bride in that white lace dress, I was struck by the lack of light in her face, or many of the women's faces, and how she barely moved. The men danced and laughed into the night, while the women huddled, and I never saw her smile. Her face, her eyes haunted me—I kept asking my boyfriend, *why wasn't she happy? Why wasn't the bride happy? Did she know her groom? What was going on?* I felt crazed by the vision of her.

Art school was knocking the creativity right out of me, and my boss kept raising my quotas. One morning not long after calling on the Great Lady, I woke up feeling there was nothing left to draw, and that I didn't want to call on any clients for work, and I was shocked at my boyfriend's indifference in my discovery and his lack of desire to talk about it. A breakfast at which he looked over the newspaper at me—as if, "what's the big deal about all this?" did the trick. Within a few weeks of Her claim on my life, I made a choice— or rather, the choice made me. I would leave the city. I would move home to the mountain, in Anderson Valley, hours from here, into the forests and creeks of my family. A tiny Airstream trailer awaited me, with no toilet or hot running water.

I was supposed to drive up with my boyfriend at the wheel—but in a sudden change of heart, right before we were going to leave, I just got in and drove away. I've always wondered what he thought in that moment! I remember driving my U-Haul across the Golden Gate Bridge, which was no small act for me, since I hadn't driven in years, living in the city. "Born to Be Wild" was playing on the radio, and I was singing and crying with the windows rolled down. I felt exuberant.

I drove more than three hours in giddy jubilance about what was coming next and about my great escape. When I got to the mountain, my mom and my mentor, Sue Hoya Sellars, were supposed to greet me after my long voyage, but no one was there. It was a black night, and the winding roads of Highway 128 had taxed my new driving skills. The magnitude of my choice set in and I had no flashlight on a moonless November night. After sitting in the dark listening to the cooling engine pop and waiting for them to come any minute and no idea where to even look for them, I opened my laptop to write and pass the time until they found me. I used the light to walk into the trailer and crawled under the covers of the bed that I knew my mother had made for me. This was the genesis of my new and future life, of driving and sometimes running, toward the feminine. Somehow landing there in the dark after such a bright city life heralded the sovereignty from all systems I had known. (It turns out my mom and Sue had been at the movies and were surprised at how fast I arrived.)

I was at Terra Sophia, twenty acres that members of my family had moved to during the women's movement and "back to the land" exodus. This space was to provide a safe haven for women. *I was one of the ones that it provided that for.* I lived on the land, ran naked through woods, wore flowers in my hair, grew my armpit hair, did juice fasts, put my menstrual blood into clay, and explored my art with fresh insights. I prayed, chanted, and asked openly for the Mother of All to speak to me, through me, and She did, in a way that I could understand—through my creativity and nature.

"She is a tree of life to those who embrace her."

~Proverbs 3:18

Sue was to be the steward of many of initiations, and it was as if she had been waiting for me since the beginning of time. She was already into the Goddess and had been for some time. Slowly, I began to find the connection between Mary and the Goddesses that Sue seemed to know all about. Many women, including my mother, contributed to this awakening—poets, artists, lesbians, witches, redheads, lawyers, and authors.

It was the beginning of the Internet era, and at the time I had no way to "search" the web for evidence of Her … that wouldn't come until years later. But I read books that explained how images of the feminine had been created for 250,000 years and how the suppression of her image was systematic, intentional, and enforced by those in charge of the telling of his-story. I began to see the threads of how Her not being a part of the lives of men and women had allowed for a patriarchal construct to dominate. And most of us had no idea. Thank our lucky stars for the female archaeologists who challenged the system and the authors who pointed out the distinctions between the chalice and the blade.

"Holy Wisdom, Soaring Power, encompass us with wings unfurled, and carry us, encircling all, above, below, and through the world."

~Hildegard of Bingen

My days were spent in a paradox between sweet discovery and rage. She was here, is here, and has always been here. My Mother, The Divine Mother, hadn't gone anywhere; she had been hidden from me and from the world religions. Even those who honored the feminine in some way—including many Goddess stories, had the feminine as secondary, and consort. Sue taught me to question even theologies that included her—Father Sky/Mother Earth Krishna/Rhadarani, Buddha/Tara, Isis/Osiris, Persephone/Hades, Shiva/Shakti, and so on. She even taught me to re-examine ideas about the sacred masculine and feminine and to reject most of what I learned and to discover it for myself. At the time and now, I valued the Christ story that had a mother and a child, but not a consort relationship. And that His closest female disciple, Magdalena, was who He chose to teach the Gospel upon rising from the dead. I wondered about this tradition that had been so distorted and if we had somehow missed the real-life boat to which He and His mother had tried to give us access.

I saw how invested world systems are in us not knowing about Her and in distorting Her image and teachings. I explored impossible ideas such as misogyny, and Sue taught me to bring the unthinkable emotional experience into art to work it out. We carved wood and dug clay. We chopped wood and carried water. I studied deeply, often in despair, in her studio on the hill. (Today, that studio is still used by our community, where we paint our cosmic feminine archetypes inspired by Sue's teachings about humans "cooling sacks of stars with our cosmic address being our body.")

In the coming weeks and months, many initiations took place—of which I will share just a few threads. Through my devotion and relationship with Her, I got almost instant access to places in my heart that I didn't know existed, intuition began to fire, brain synapses began to increase their functionality in very insightful potent revelations, and love itself, along with the rage, was expanded exponentially. Could it be that before Her, I was just living out a fraction of the potential self? It certainly seemed so. She opened me to the field around my body, my brain, and my capacity to be conscious by choice.

One of the initiations that took place some weeks into my mountain mama experience was my choice to not to talk about God in the masculine for one year. To just not say "God." To reframe my thinking and discover a way to really be with Her. I stood on a mountaintop, faced the open sky, and spoke another time, to the Father and Son. I told them I would be back but that for now I need to deepen and know the Mothers. My pronouncement was followed by waiting to be struck dumb or by lightening—but I lived, and lived to tell about it too. That fear of honoring the feminine and confronting the masculine ideas was so prevalent that I felt I might just die from speaking it! I wondered how many other women felt this way. I also told Father and Son that I would maintain the flame of Christ—but genderless for the time being. I had to find my way without the continual reaction of the patriarchy hogging all the sacred space within my psyche.

Even with all of this, I was a frustrated artist and found myself wondering if I should just quit art altogether. This day I was praying in line drawings … and suddenly there it was, as if my hand had finally found the groove it was seeking. I made circles upon circles, mamas within mamas with babies—eggs within eggs, and it was fluid and free, and, me. I cried. I am crying now as I write this. I remember feeling that the moment was holy. Sue was out milking the goats, and I ran and showed it to her. I was suddenly afraid I wouldn't be able to do it again. But I did. And again, and again for twenty-five years, and made my entire living and called my entire community, from those circles upon circles. Sue always talked about "finding one's own way of working." My mother saw my little drawings and called them "original and brilliant." I had found it, found my way of working. Finally, the art began to pour through me. For the first time, I felt I had found my own voice. I was ecstatic. This felt different than anything I had ever experienced or created. Those drawings a few years later would go into my first book, a coloring book called "Color of Woman."

I began to make art about Her, to Her, as offerings. Another day, I was trying to bring what I was experiencing in drawing into painting, but it wasn't happening. I was frustrated for weeks on the transition from page to canvas. Sue, seeing my obvious desperation, said, "Let's try this." I can see her hand on the canvas now—floating purple, yellow and green with a spray bottle of water onto a 16x20 canvas. She handed me the brush, I then made the few strokes—a black Madonna and child emerged out of the cosmos. I had found my way to Her. The joy I felt in my soul began to weave my anger into a potent vision for the future. I had to tell others about Her, about this … but I wasn't ready yet.

I had endless conversations with my mother about scripture and the feminine—so understanding was she that she even showed me where to find the mother in those pages. Her genius, patience, and comprehension about what I was experiencing kept me on the path of including Christ along the way. As it turns out, when she was pregnant with me, she and Sue had decided to leave the patriarchy altogether. Mom later returned, Sue never did, and I was to be the weave of both worlds. I felt Jesus has given us His Mother, and She had given us Him, and yet, we missed it. We missed it.

"Here is your mother."

~John 19:26

With clay from the land, I fashioned my little round goddesses, as I imagined the women's hands shaping Venus of Wilendorf. I imagined women sitting around the fire making her in their own image. As I made art, I made myself. Perhaps I was being formed by Her hands. I felt a passion for restoring the image of the feminine to the face of the earth through the hands of women who loved Her. At this point in history it was time for *herstory*. A new vision emerged for me: We would remake Her in our image and we would be unstoppable—and impossible to hide.

There would be so many of us making her image that we would take the world by storm. And we have. We truly have, as our worldwide community of women artists reaches into the tens of thousands. Our homes, our offices, our sanctuaries, our shelters, our hospitals, our jails, our galleries, our schools are filling with Her, created by the hands of women exploring Her for themselves. The Divine Mother doesn't seem to mind populating Herself in thousands of colors and names and outfits and adornments—and teachings.

I had so many breakthroughs it seems sometimes like the rest of my life has been about living them out. I remember one day as I stood in the studio wedging clay that we had taken weeks and weeks to dig and prepare, I complained to Sue, "Can't we just buy clay at the store? Do we have to make it ourselves? It is so long in between making it and throwing the pot, I just want to make a bowl on the wheel." She then said the words my soul came to earth to hear, the words that I live by today. I remember the sound of her spoon stirring in her cup of tea, and coming to a stop. I can smell the crackling fire and see the shades of lemon yellow light streaming through spider webs in the window behind her.

And she said: "What do you care about seeing changed in the world?"

"I care about ending violence for women and their children."

"Put that into the clay. Wedge your intention into the clay as you work. Believe it is being sent and received by the women and children now, because, it is."

Later that day, after I was satisfied with having thrown my first pots on the wheel, she told me about monks who meditated being able to decrease violence in a city somewhere. And she told me about her mentor and guardian, Lenore Thomas Straus, about how Lenore had approached her stone sculpting as if the stone had presence and consciousness and how she worked for Eleanor Roosevelt as one of the New Deal artists. She told me about Michelangelo and his belief that the image was in the stone and his job was to reveal it. She told me about women singing to end war. We went way back, to Catal Huyuk and the caves of Lascaux and she showed me how our people have been telling stories in art since time began. This was the beginning of the worldwide movement I would steward in a conscious way, rooted in what would come to be called Intentional Creativity.

I asked myself ... What story would I tell? What story would my art tell about our people in this era? What is mine to share? What was I here to cause and create? What did I want others to know about Her? My year of mentorship on the mountain held all the ingredients that I would continue to live into the rest of my life, so far.

This journey to this point was not without suffering; perhaps any true initiation requires the stuff of vision questions. Through my awakening to Her and my own art came awareness about the suffering of the women in the world. Those moments when you know that murder and birth and love making are all happening at the same moment—yes, one of those experiences of the collective human condition: *"How could anyone be conscious of the suffering in the world, especially that which is inflicted on women and live?"* Her "voice" arises like an occurring within me, not like a sound of a voice but a distinct and clear knowing of something other than my own voice. It was in answer to the prayer of my heart: *"I will give you what you need. And one day you will give it all away. Then I will give you something else."* This moment was the advent of realizing my art was not for me but for the world. For women. For Her. And that it didn't really belong to me, but was coming through me but on behalf of others.

The transition of it not being all about me and my process and my relationship to Her—to it being about loving others and a life of service—

changed the energy and how I was holding it. My life was now an offering on the altar of creation.

During this cycle, many wise woman teachers came and contributed to my inquiries and struggles. Our neighbor, the author Alice Walker, came for tea with Sue, and they talked in depth about the status of women. It was the time when we were learning about female genital mutilation. In a gulping teary conversation I asked if women would ever be safe. Alice replied, *"Women are not safe anywhere."* Somehow the acknowledgment of this was a comfort to me—to just say it, to name it, to know it and to begin to explore it for myself. And to be in resolve about what my part would be in tending the end of violence against women in any way that I could. I didn't know, of course, what that would look like; now I do, but then I was in the mystery. I remembered the bride from Somalia and I understood why she didn't smile. I committed that I would do my part, for her and for the checkout girls, and for anyone who didn't have a voice, or the privilege of a chance to discover their voice.

At the end of that year of study of art and Her, I had a body of work. Sue suggested it was time to have an art opening, a show—my first art show! I had pottery with carvings and beads, poetry, photographs with acrylic transfer of my drawings, painted egg forms, wood sculpture, and paintings. All were Her, and many had her little son in her arms, and many had a great Mama of All enfolding all of them. The show was a success—it was a sold-out show. The Christian story mythos wove its way back in through art … but this time with my awareness of the feminine. I would not go anywhere without my Mother.

> "Does not wisdom call out? Does not
> understanding raise her voice?"
>
> *~Proverbs 8:1*

My story of my relationship with Mother as my teacher has continued on from there in mighty and mysterious was. She remains for me the Blessed Mother, the Goddess of this current paradigm, available to all who seek Her. From my relationship with Her, the being that I am, was able to come into fullness, a ripening that continues. When we are walking the earth and have no sense of self connected with the Divine Mother, any of the

Divine Mothers, we see ourselves as outcasts, not part of the "real story" and secondary to the masculine. The problem with this is obvious: First, it is a lie. And, second it holds us in subjugation. And, finally, not knowing we are Her and part of Her may even keep us from the greatness of our own intelligence. My experience was that she held the keys to my very consciousness, that connection with Her filled in the blanks of womanhood and created the story of my incredible life. I also saw that without Her, even men aren't able to reach their potential.

> "I love those who love me, and those
> who seek me find me."
>
> *~Proverbs 8:17*

Years later I would return to including the masculine as part of my personal faith walk and not feel rage but compassion. When I returned, I came wrapped in Her garment of red threads. That day at worship the feeling started that "something was very wrong" and has continued to be a theme woven into my life. Any place or space where women are not honored as truly equal and part of the Divine has fault in my view.

I will continue to take a stand, for Her.

Shiloh Sophia lives life as a great adventure! She is a renaissance woman who communicates her philosophy through paintings, poetry, teachings and entrepreneurship. For twenty-five years she has dedicated her soul work to the study and practice of creativity as a path of healing that provides access to consciousness. As a curator and gallery owner, she has represented her own work, as well as hundreds of women artists. By the age of forty she had achieved incredible success through being in the top 10 percent of sales for contempo-  rary artists in the United States. Her prolific intuitive painting process led to a desire to teach and provided the foundation for the groundbreaking work on how Intentional Creativity® can give voice to the soul. Her method of "Creating with mindfulness" has reached tens of thousands of students who have gained insight into the hidden self. Her work is taught widely, at universities in master's and doctoral programs, the United Nations CSW, and by hundreds of Certified Teachers and Coaches. At the core of her work is a belief that the right to self-express is one of the most basic human rights—"We have a right to know how to access what we think, feel, believe and to express it in our lives." Her life path is a spiritual practice and an offering that was awakened with the feminine Divine. Her research dives into the exploration of the right/left brain connection with the heart and re-inventing personal archetypes as gateways to liberation. She is the creator of seven books as well as a community leader. Having been trained by her mother Caron McCloud the poet, and Sue Hoya Sellars the artist, she brought her gifts of language and image into form through founding the Intentional Creativity® Guild, Cosmic Cowgirls®, Power Creatives TV and Color of Woman®. She lives and works at Cosmic Cowgirls Ranch in Sonoma, California, which provides education both in-house and online, reaching over 25,000 subscribers a month. She can be found most days having tea with her muses discussing quantum physics and celebrating revelations of the heart. Learn more: **www.shilohsophia.com**

Birthing Civilization 2.0

BY SAMANTHA SWEETWATER

I was conceived on a riverbank. Sunburned and steaming green, I was made in love. I was not chosen, but when my mother discovered she was pregnant, she and my father said yes. She walked away from a budding career as a textile designer to become a mom. He set aside his art to become a college administrator. My earliest memories are of the comfort of my parents' arms and of the overwhelming terror of collective annihilation. Even as a tiny child, I could feel the storm coming. Somehow, I was born with a presentient awareness of systems collapse. This has shaped every moment of my life.

When I was fifteen, I was raped. I snuck off campus with a big, tall blonde senior. I remember his blue eyes and his bravado. I think he was the captain of the football team. I recall being smitten by his flirtatious charm, good looks and obvious status. He drove us to a park and found a shady spot in trees at the back of the lot. He got me laughing, and plied me with hard liquor. Being completely unfamiliar with alcohol, I was smashed before I knew it. Once I was too drunk to resist, he pinned me down and finger fucked me. I hardly remember him dropping me off at home. I was in such shock. It took me twenty years to reclaim my virginity. And, I've never been drunk again.

In November 2016, I was in South Africa during Donald Trump's inauguration. From that vantage point, far on the other side of the planet, it was obvious that a sociopathic rapist had captured not only America but the world. I sat on the porch of the guest house nestled against tall red mountains, glued to CNN. I talked for hours with my hosts about the emergence of a global culture of cynicism, domination and fear, and how Trump's rise gave permission to the worst behavior of other such rulers around the globe. We could all see him as the most obvious figurehead in the rise of an ultimate pathology in our world. The whole world was sick that day. And heartbroken. His inauguration marked the crossing of a threshold from bad to baddest with Trump as the perfect archetype of an extreme form of unfeeling masculine domination that is the inevitable result of disconnection from the feminine and from the earth.

AN INVITATION

Dear Sisters,

Can we set aside easy and do some real women's work? Would you walk with me through the Eye of the Needle? Would you dedicate your leadership to our children's future? Would you be still with me to make space within yourself for the harmonics of Oneness with Life? Would you let yourself fall apart to unleash the debt of grief that makes us worthy to praise what we love? Would you disrobe the naked majesty of your soul? Would you dance and cry and stay the long days and nights with me as we work collectively to heal our species and our world? And, would you pray? Would you settle into the soft animal of you and amplify your prayers through the limitless power of your open heart?

I need this from you. We need it from each other.

From here, we can know each other authentically. We can know each other as true humans. We can be a power of togetherness, no longer power under or over. We can balance the impossible over-fullness of contemporary living as we cobble a tapestry of soul-in-bodies, aligning the Universal Purpose to care for and tend the Earth with the rainbow of power unleashed when each of us makes manifest our Unique Purpose and gifts.

As I write these words, I am surrounded with the easeful peace of a beautiful summer day. Birds sing. Distant cars and trains make music as wind chimes sing softly in the breeze. I drink a glass of pure ice water to keep cool. But, do not be deceived. Nothing is normal.

This is a most non-ordinary time.

We are at the end. We are at a beginning. Science is proving Spirit in Matter as consciousness expands. Yet, limits are pushing. The planet groans under the sheer volume of human life. We already have technology sufficient to solve our worst problems, yet AI, CRISPR gene editing technology, readily available nuclear capacity and other technological mechanisms could destroy all in a blink. Climate change and overpopulation guarantee runaway cycles that are already pretty much out of control. And, we can no longer count on world leaders to take care of people or the planet.

WHAT'S A GIRL TO DO?

It's time to get dirty and feisty and step up to the plate.

Being a woman and a leader in these times necessitates raw presence with immensely complex inevitabilities and potentialities that aren't pretty. They are about as scary as it gets, they are directly on the horizon, and they challenge us to stay sane and focused even in the face of existential nihilism, depression, meaninglessness, fear, loss, injustice, hatred and greed. These conditions demand wisdom. Stay open. Don't flinch.

Let yourself be shattered. You can't love the world into wholeness if you can't let it break your heart.

Choose to heal and to be a healer. I shared the stories above because these are the experiences we have to face, embrace and transcend in order to heal. They are systemic, and blaming anyone will get us nowhere fast. You need to *know* that forgiveness is your #1 superpower. If you aren't already extremely good at the alchemy held in the words "thank you; I love you; please forgive me," then it's time to fully establish that habit and skill. We have all lived through rape, or its equivalent. Being a victim just leads to more perpetration, and we can't afford that pendulum swing anymore.

Lead and love in alignment with your soul. Because, while your body, your heart and your head are all brilliant and powerful centers of intelligence, they each have their own ways of perceiving and connecting to the world, and they are all fallible. (Yes, even your heart.) But, *your soul* is an impeccable rudder for the highest and truest direction of your life. It is the part of yourself you can trust to steer your incarnation impulse, your desires, your creativity and what you choose to say no or yes to, with immaculate precision relative to your place in the greater ecology of consciousness, creation and human endeavor. Being a woman leader means being soul-centric at all costs.

Own your pleasure. Your pleasure is a beacon, an evolutionary principle and an insurance policy that guarantees that your impulses and your actions align with Life. If it's not pleasurable, on some level, it's probably a denial of life. Pleasure is its own reward. If you can't own this, you've already lost the game.

A feminine evolutionary leader isn't born leading. She is born caring. She is born loving. Through this love, she finds that she must lead. "She" may not even be a woman. She may be a man, or a person of another gender, enacting his own feminine. Feminine leadership is for all people who lead through love.

ARE YOU IN?

Awesome ... I thought so. Okay. It's time to ask hard questions and be with hard problems.

The hard questions sound something like this:

How do we finally heal root trauma and the ongoing problems of poverty, racism, sexism, climate change, and a host of other ethical, social, ecological, political crises in our world? Can we release and recode unconscious entitlement and greed? How can we build a culture that empowers celebration and grief at the same time? Can we re-wild ourselves and relearn deep collaboration with nature? What is right action when the stakes are so high? What ancient/future design principles will support us to co-orchestrate a return to harmony for ourselves and our planet?

The hard problem looks something like this:

We can't keep going the way we have and survive. Period.

This is the truth. Our lives and leadership in the next five years will make or break the future of the human project and all other species on our home Earth.

A RADICAL PROPOSAL

It's time to live the answers. It's time to crash Civilization as we know it while we simultaneously reboot it at a new octave of coherency. It's time to build Civilization 2.0. We play the primal roles of midwives and hospice workers as we tend the birth and steward a death that's been needing to happen for a long time.

You are a powerful contributor. Please bring your gifts and talents, your unique knowledge and perspective, your particular web of impact, intimacy and influence, and your radiant, embodied woman self. Please bring your business, your family, your friends, your community, and the places you call home. This is about restoring intimacy and belonging—in all of these spheres—in a regenerative planetary culture of peace. This may sound impossible, but it's not. Systemically, it's already happening. Each step weaves an ever-deeper fabric of the prayer. It's both the right thing to do and the beautiful thing to do. It's the only thing that makes sense.

What is Civilization 2.0? It's an emergent pattern for the human project rooted in coherent systems design that is in integrity with nature and the soul. It's the natural evolution of the Anthropocene—a planetary emergence that transcends and includes what has come before, integrating everything we have learned at a new octave of belonging, coherency and love. It's Feminine at its core. It is in dynamic and ever-changing equilibrium with the Masculine. It's all and both.

Civilization 2.0 is what our world will be when we are no longer pathological to our own survival. It's what the whole human project, including economy, technology and governance, will behave like when we design systems that are net regenerative in every sector of life. It's what our world will feel like when all people have access to food, water, shelter, and basic health care and are guaranteed the freedoms to learn, create, celebrate and pray. It's how meaning and value will be exchanged and defined when we return to a basic co-creativity with Nature. It's who we will know ourselves to be as we learn to inhabit our human nature as a true, co-creative expression *of* Nature, Soul and of Source.

Civilization 2.0 is truly the "rise of the divine feminine" in its most functional form—a systemic and all-encompassing expression of human endeavor and worldview within which each of our lives is aligned with our earth mother, and the design within our souls that knows we each have a role to play in the larger ecology of consciousness and soul. It's a full-circle return to an ancient indigenous way of knowing that understands that we are not separate from the hoop of life, and that reciprocity is law of the land. It's a net-indigenous worldview, grounded in restored belonging to place, that now it includes our awareness of ourselves as global, galactic and universal citizens.

As a leader in Civilization 2.0, you get to know yourself as an incarnated being whose evolutionary role is to co-create ever greater harmony and complexity in the universe. From the Goddess's perspective, this is why you're here. Civilization 2.0 is a way of describing your life when you align with your soul's true design and the Original Instructions your soul already knows.

How can we recode the very fabric of civilization? By living loud, large, bright and true, but also through a deeper alchemy that cannot be ignored. We have to reach down into the darkest substrate of our trauma. We have to wind our ways down into the deepest pain of our epigenetic wounding, our family traumas, our community disruptions, and our failure to belong to specific places on the Earth. We have to reach up, into a greater expanse of our consciousness to know ourselves as homo luminous—at home on our planet and in the universe—for the first time. And, we have to be willing to let things die.

All of this has never been done before. But, we are the ones to do it, with feminine intelligence embedded in the root codes, and women strongly and visibly in the lead. We collaborate with everything: existing power structures and systems, men, children, elders, plants, animals, ancestors and the unseen, to weave wisdom and belonging. We are starting to understand that our freedom is interdependent with our responsibility to all that is. Real feminine evolutionary intelligence is an intelligence of oneness and connection. It embraces everything. Nothing is not included in this win-win game.

ROOT CODE: BELONGING AND LISTENING

From the goddess' perspective, She is alive, awake and manifest in everything. She is a fabric of immanence. She is Life itself. She co-births herself through the omniscient and omnipresent intelligence of all that is, and the pure mind of transcendent Source. She's a badass who's all about being *here* and being *now*. In the Goddess' eyes, nothing is not sacred. And, if you aren't able to feel and know your membership to and with and through the world as the juicy reality where the sacred is manifest, you're not there yet.

You belong to the world and it belongs to you. You are two parts of the one goddess dancing in delighted individuation and oneness. You are a Me in communion with the We in communion with the One all at the same time.

In a Feminine worldview, you get to be in conversation as everything. Everything informs and shapes you. You think in terms of wholes and relationships, not in terms of parts. This is the heart of shamanism, tantra and other truly non-dual perspectives. And, it needs to be the center of our way of creating ethics and educating our children, if we want to help them create a world that works for Life.

How do you make it real? You learn how to listen. Learn how to talk to the world as though it were listening. Pray, dance, have a conversation with a spider. Create businesses, technologies and educational frameworks that are responsive to and respectful of the Life in things. Incentivize win-win and balance. Assume change.

In case your ability to listen has been acculturated or beaten out of you (as our schools, churches and often our well intending parents do their best to do), here's a little instruction on you restore your ability to listen:

Talk to things as if you expect they will respond to you. Open your mouth and begin an earnest conversation. Suspend your disbelief. Disbelief inhibits the potential you are seeking to open up. Shift your perspective from that of "objective" observer to subjective participant taking a witness stance.

Fill your stance with curiosity. "I wonder ... How are you, fig tree? You are beautiful. Do you like that new lavender bush I planted?" Assume, for a moment, that the thing is responding, even if you can't hear it. Assume that the purpose of your existence is to be in relationship with the rest of existence and get curious about how it speaks to you.

The goddess plays the game of consciousness by granting Life to all things. This is a pleasurable game. Welcome to the conversation.

When you learn to listen, you become a good follower. By becoming a good follower, you become worthy to lead.

ORIGINAL INSTRUCTIONS

There is something you know way deep inside you. It was nearly extinguished, but somewhere, way behind all the schooling and layers of culture, beneath all the generations of trauma and forgetting, on the other side of a gray wall of forgetting, lies and deception, you have a memory of what you are really here for.

Your Original Instructions, as a biological being who may have come from the stars, and certainly co-evolved with this planet, are to tend and steward the well-being of all species and all living systems on this earth.

Your Original instructions have always been here. They are braided into your genetics. They are a Universal Purpose that runs alongside your unique Personal Purpose. They are bio-logical. To follow them is to unlock pleasure, genius and co-creativity that aligns perfectly with the organism of you—your body, your nervous system, your health. They are erotic. The space where your deep listening and your soul's creativity meets the calling of the world is a kiss, a hot, wet, magical kiss that can make dreams manifest and bring truth, goodness and beauty to life.

You can learn Original Instructions through nature immersion, prayer and ceremony, by learning through biomimicry or by telling stories. If you are willing to give the time and attention, you can easily read them in the Book of Nature. They are constantly whispering, sometimes screaming. You will hear them clearly if you are willing to attend to your pains and pleasures, to your unbound curiosity in relationship to your body and nature, to the voices of Ancestors, to Gaia and to Source. You will embody them when you unleash and tune your instinct, intuition, empathic, psychic and intuitive senses.

After all, you co-evolved with this planet. The instructions are so obvious in the design that we've overlooked them. It's absolutely antithetical to your own well-being to destroy the environment that nourishes you. The earth is, literally, your mother. Your instructions are to be good children. It's no different than any family. To lead is both to create the space for your inner prodigal child to return, and to hold space and craft stories that help the rest of humanity to do the same.

OUR CHOICE

Feminine evolutionary leadership is a radical necessity. If we are going to lead evolution, we need to take really seriously that our evolution is itself at stake, and we have to ask ourselves what it would take to lead our species in such a way that evolution actually continues, for us and our children and all other beings on this planet. We have to ask ourselves if we're willing to take the essence of the feminine so seriously that we fall heart-crackingly in love with all that is such that we are unable to deny our fundamental interconnectivity with the world.

It's time to stop getting lost in transcendent spirituality and to come down to earth, hard, right into our hearts and our bodies and the immense messy problem of our species so that we can inhabit radical duty. This duty is the fundament of our freedom as feminine beings, because feminine freedom is based first and foremost on belonging, not on getting what you want or being able to inhabit liberation in a transcendent space, but in the messy process of being fully expressed and connected here, in the world, where the feminine is alive and well and making itself all the time.

Any movement of feminine empowerment that polarizes from the masculine or from men is destined to recreate victim/perpetrator dynamics and politics of separation and specific interest at the expense of someone else. Any movement of women's empowerment that positions men as non-feminine beings is destined to recreate unnecessary battles between the sexes and alienation between people whose internal masculine/feminine balance and unique capacities and skills are otherwise perfectly designed for collaboration. We need everybody on deck, now. And we need to be the kind of people who can empower that kind of radical participation, for all beings, none excluded.

So, put your masculine in service to the Feminine. Put your feminine in service to everything. Celebrate your masculine as a superpower of structure, and integrate it into your ever-more radiant, loving, authentic and soul-centric walk in the world.

Because, what the world needs now is women who have come fully alive. The world needs women who fiercely belong to the world. Women who have come fully alive have the capacity to bring the world alive, to bring children alive, to bring men alive, to bring the Earth alive and to bring themselves alive, even as we walk together into the what will undoubtedly be the most chaotic time in human memory. We walk together. We walk in joy. We walk in commitment. We walk in love.

Mentor, author, shaman, dance artist and wisdompreneur, **Samantha Sweetwater** *is a pioneering guide of embodied transformation, soul-aligned leadership and nature connection. As a wayshower, innovator and community co-creator, she has invested over twenty years into the emergence of a global, regenerative culture of peace. She designs experiences that heal, reveal and celebrate our fundamental belonging to self, family, community and place, engaging participants at the intersections of somatics, shamanism, neuroscience, integral theory, ancient wisdom, biomimicry and art. As a mentor, she partners with individuals and organizations to activate both the Unique Purpose inherent in each soul and the Universal Purpose we all carry as human beings to co-create evolutionary harmony with All of Life. She is well known as the former Founder (and current Spiritual Director) of the global movement of www.DancingFreedom.com™ and the co-founder of the PeaceBody School Japan. Through these vehicles, she has trained hundreds of facilitators and touched tens of thousands of lives on six continents. Her current projects include the RESIDENCE: Body, Love and Leadership in the Age of Belonging, www.LivingWisdomRetreats.com, offering immersive, initiatory experiences for high impact leaders in extraordinary places globally, and One Life Circle, an intimate space for community healing and prayer held monthly in the Bay Area. Learn more:* **www.SamanthaSweetwater.com**

PHOTO BY WARWICK SAINT

Fortunate Failing

BY ARIEL WHITE

Standing before myself
With sheer recklessness and curiosity
Devouring my essence with hungry jowls
Glistening in saliva, oily and sweet

Beckoning my last saving grace
Coming from total destruction
I fly alone in your embrace

Ripping my heart out
Remembering it is only breath
I offer you
My pulse

The ocean of my Yoni in rhythmic spanda*
Rising and falling
I am the infinite bridge
Coursing with Life

Hollow bones
Lit with rainbow radiance
Death's wife ... Death's wife

My womb vibrates in delight
Tasting anew the miraculous
spice of night
Abandoning only what
keeps me "safe"

Playing it all away
And I know—nothing
Soaring. Courageous.
Naked.

Bellowing a melodic cry
An ode to the totality of my
deep dance
With all that's sacred and
profane

I reclaim my name:
Lioness of Gaia
Everything to gain
By failing in clinging to
limitless space

She touches my face
An ocean of air
Awaiting my breath
Reminding me

Be still in the chaos
Make Love
To the (I) of the storm

~Ariel White

* Spanda means "tremor" or "vibration" and is the primordial vibration of our being and the universe

Ariel White *is an artist, entrepre-*
neur, and facilitator of women's wis-
dom. Founder of Amant.co, a digital
media company for Lovers, Ariel brings
together art, products, and messages
that support women in feeling beautiful,
well-pleasured, and sensually expressed.
Ariel has been in the fields of somatic
and sex-education for over a decade,
leading retreats and teaching interna-
tionally to women from over thirty coun-
tries, spanning from Malaysia to Necker
Island. Creator of MyLittleYoni.com,
each unique "Yoni Doll" is a symbol

and tool for women's sexual healing and celebration of their feminine nature. My
Little Yoni a symbol helping to create a post-patriarchal world, where women are
connected to the unique, creative power of their vagina. Ariel has a deep love for
poetry and the quality of presence invoked through spoken-word and music. For
close to a decade she has invested into sustainable community land projects, with
a strong desire to reinvent the village. She splits her time between Los Angeles and
Kauai, bridging earth wisdom with empowering media. Ariel feels honored to be
included in the Feminine Evolution project and prays that women worldwide find
their voice and claim their sovereignty. Follow Ariel on instagram: @MyLittleYoni
and @Amant.co

Additional Flower of Life Press Books
available on Amazon.com

Path of the Priestess: Discover Your Divine Purpose

Sacred Call of the Ancient Priestess: Birthing a New Feminine Archetype

Rise Above: Free Your Mind One Brushstroke at a Time

Menopause Mavens: Master the Mystery of Menopause

The Power of Essential Oils: Create Positive Transformation in Your Well-being, Business, and Life

Self-Made Wellionaire: Get Off Your Ass(et), Reclaim Your Health, & Feel Like a Million Bucks

Oms From the Mat: Breathe, Move, & Awaken to the Power of Yoga

Oms From the Heart: Open Your Heart to the Power of Yoga

The Four Tenets of Love: Open, Activate, & Inspire Your Life's Path

Made in the USA
San Bernardino, CA
24 September 2017